Spirit
Capture

Spirit Capture

PHOTOGRAPHS FROM
THE NATIONAL MUSEUM
OF THE AMERICAN INDIAN

EDITED BY TIM JOHNSON

PUBLISHED BY SMITHSONIAN INSTITUTION PRESS
IN ASSOCIATION WITH
THE NATIONAL MUSEUM OF THE AMERICAN INDIAN
SMITHSONIAN INSTITUTION
WASHINGTON AND LONDON

Cover: Oneida family portrait, 1907. Ontario, Canada. Photo by Mark R. Harrington. N2641

Inside front cover:
Gelatin silver print of Alompum and Tax-a-lax (Cayuse), twin grandnieces of Chief Joseph, born February 1898. Photo by Lee Moorhouse, 2 October 1898. P10361

Title page:
Portrait of three Alaska Eskimo (Inuit) girls, ca. 1900. Photo by Lomen Brothers. N35407

Inside back cover:
Gelatin silver print of Alompum and Tax-a-lax (Cayuse), twin grandnieces of Chief Joseph, born February 1898. Photo by Lee Moorhouse, 2 October 1898. P10362

Back cover:
Bernice Begay (Navajo) and Bah Chee (Navajo), mother and daughter, 16 May 1981. Jeddito Island, Arizona. © Toba P. Tucker. P23390

Published in conjunction with an exhibition that will open in early 1999 at the National Museum of the American Indian, George Gustav Heye Center, Alexander Hamilton U.S. Custom House, New York City.

Library of Congress Cataloging-in-Publication Data
Spirit capture: photographs from the National Museum of the American Indian / edited by Tim Johnson.
     p.   cm.
    Includes bibliographical references and index.
    ISBN 1-56098-924-6 (cloth : alk. paper). — ISBN 1-56098-765-0 (paper : alk. paper)
    I. Indians of North America—Pictorial works. 2. Indians—Pictorial works. 3. Photography in ethnology. 4. National Museum of the American Indian (U.S.) I. Johnson, Tim, 1947– . II. National Museum of the American Indian (U.S.)
E77.5.S65   1998
779'.997000497—dc21   98-4173

Spirit Capture is published with the assistance of a grant from the Smithsonian Women's Committee.

Terence Winch: Head of publications and project director
Cheryl Wilson: Project manager
Nancy Eickel: Editor
Lou Stancari: Photo editor
Linda McKnight: Designer
Typeset in Monotype Centaur

Printed in Italy, at no government expense.

The National Museum of the American Indian, Smithsonian Institution, is dedicated to working in collaboration with the indigenous peoples of the Americas to foster and protect Native cultures throughout the Western Hemisphere. The museum's publishing program seeks to augment awareness of Native American beliefs and lifeways, and to educate the public about the history and significance of Native cultures.

Seneca girl, ca. 1910. Photo by

Alanson B. Skinner. N1706

Cochiti Pueblo family, ca. 1920.

Photo by Odd S. Halseth. N32987

Contents

Akawoia fisherman calling to his
prey, 1917. British Guiana. Photo by
A. Hyatt Verrill. N10100

Foreword

Cultural "truths," I firmly believe, are created by those telling the story. Let me give a few examples. In 1877, one William Jackson compiled a volume entitled *Descriptive Catalogue of Photographs of North American Indians.* This catalogue contains a photograph of an Apache man named Eskiminzin, who is described in the following way:

> Height, 5 feet 8 inches; circumference of head, 22¼ inches; circumference of chest, 37 inches; age, 38 years. Head chief of San Carlos reservation and of the Pinal Apaches. His family was among those slain at the Camp Grant massacre in 1871. Is now taking the lead in living a civilized life, having taken up a farm on the San Carlos River.

Whatever Eskiminzin might have thought about "civilized life" on his San Carlos River farm, I have always had great difficulty believing that if you asked him who he was and what was important to him, he would have responded by telling you the circumference of his head and chest.

Let me give another illustration of this kind of cultural relativity from my own personal experience. Once, as a child, I was sitting with a much older Indian man, the two of us leafing through a book of photographs by Edward S. Curtis, whose elegant works continue to be so enormously popular. I was as mesmerized as a seven-year-old could be by the handsome, often panoramic photographic visions and their gentle sepia tones. When I remarked how much I liked the pictures, my elderly companion dispatched my youthful and apparently undiscriminating admiration by noting gruffly, "It was nothing like that."

I was puzzled at the time since, for a seven-year-old, a photograph represented visual fact rather than opinion, and was supposed to be objective rather than subjective. In the intervening years, however, I have appreciated the limitations of my childhood perceptions. In a profound way, Curtis imposed his own vision and understanding of reality on the subjects he

Onondaga woman and child, 1888.

Onondaga reservation, New York.

Photo by DeCost Smith. N22322

1. W. Richard West, Sr., W. Richard West, Jr., James West, Benjamin West, Christina West, and Karin West, 1992. New York, New York. Photo by Pamela Dewey.

photographed rather than reflecting what may have been their very different perceptions of that same reality.

The invention of photography, more than one-and-a-half centuries ago, was to the world's visual realities what the printing press was to language—a revolutionary technology that transformed the communication and transmission of information and knowledge. When it came to Indians, however, the Curtises and William Jacksons, and not their Native subjects, were the storytellers. The new medium rarely viewed reality through Native eyes (fig. 1). One of our most serious commitments at the National Museum of the American Indian is to offer a counterbalance to the distortions engendered by the painfully long exclusion of Indian people from the interpretation of their own history and culture. Books such as *Spirit Capture: Photographs from the National Museum of the American Indian* are crucial to our mission, for they help to set the story straight.

If there is one dimension of the vast NMAI collection that helps us to understand why we are who we are—that brings into focus, literally, the history of the Native peoples of this hemisphere—it is our incredible photographic archive. Drawing on some two hundred of the finest and most compelling pictures from among the approximately ninety thousand we are privileged to hold, and complemented by a number of arresting contemporary photos that help demonstrate the continuing vitality of Native cultures, *Spirit Capture* offers a visual narrative of Indian life and history unlike any other book with which I am familiar.

But please don't think this is a pretty picture book of "vanishing Americans." Under the imaginative and learned leadership of editor Tim Johnson, the contributors to *Spirit Capture* have given us a text that examines the complex relationship between Indians and photography from diverse perspectives, but always with keen insight and resonant wisdom. This is not a story told from the outside. The Native and non-Native contributors to this book bring to their work here not only an intimate and detailed knowledge of our collection, but also a profound understanding of Indian life and culture. Let me point briefly to one essay in this book that I think serves to illustrate the spirit of the volume as a whole. One of our contributors is Linda Poolaw, noted curator and educator, and daughter of renowned Kiowa photographer Horace Poolaw. What she does in her essay I find to be as quintessentially Indian as it is rhetorically striking: she conducts something of a dialogue with the pictures in her essay, conferring upon them a life of their own. Through the questions she puts to the people in the photographs, Poolaw indirectly gives voice to these amazing pictures. In a way, the entire book is something of a conversation between the photographs and the essayists. We invite the readers of *Spirit Capture* to become part of the conversation as well.

I am gratified to be able to offer to readers a book that successfully honors the complexity of its subject, as I believe *Spirit Capture* does. Such an accomplishment, however, would not be possible without the help of many hands. First among them is Tim Johnson, the book's guiding spirit, so to speak, and now, I'm pleased to say, a member of the NMAI staff as our new Deputy Assistant Director for Community Services. The other contributors to the book were, of course, crucial to the process: Natasha Bonilla Martinez, formerly on the staff of the Museum of the American Indian and leading authority on the NMAI photo collection; Nigel Russell, an expert on the history of photography; Rose Wyaco, a dynamic presence in the world of Native photography; Rick Hill, our former colleague and one of the most prominent and outspoken voices in contemporary Native cultural life; Linda Poolaw, a stalwart friend of the museum and a powerful teacher and writer. We are also deeply grateful to three highly regarded Native photographers— Larry Gus, Larry McNeil, and Dorothy Grandbois—for lending us their talent so that we might make clear in *Spirit Capture* that the history of Indians and photography is still being written. Finally, I am personally delighted that among the book's contributors are a group of photographers and writers from our own staff. Pam Dewey, Head of Photo Archive, photographers Katherine Fogden and Janine Sarna Jones, and former colleague Laura Nash all step out from behind the museum's backstage machinery, where most of us labor invisibly, to take a front-and-center role in this book. We also extend our thanks to Florence Shipek and Ken Taylor, Sr., for their content expertise, and to Julia Smith, who worked with our photo staff to produce the best possible prints of the images you see herein.

Everyone on our Publications staff has also worked diligently to bring this book to life. Terence Winch, Head of Publications, had the initial idea for the book and, as project director, supervised its development; project manager Cheryl Wilson attended to a myriad of details with skill and good humor; photo editor Lou Stancari applied himself, as always, with unswerving devotion to every detail; Ann Kawasaki navigated the project through seas of paperwork with her customary competence; Elizabeth Kennedy Gische helped tie up a host of loose ends. The book was also well served by the keen eye of contract editor Nancy Eickel, the efforts early in the game of former NMAI editor Holly Stewart, and by the advice of our colleagues in the Smithsonian's Office of Contracting.

To our colleagues at Smithsonian Institution Press we are also very indebted. Former Director Daniel Goodwin and former editor Amy Pastan provided an enthusiastic welcome to *Spirit Capture*. Designer Linda McKnight created a compelling context for these wonderful photos and essays. Editor Jack Kirshbaum shepherded the book through various stages of production, while production director Ken Sabol, with his trademark geniality, guided *Spirit Capture* to the finish line. Marketing director Annette Windhorn and publicist Brenda Tucker have helped ensure the book's success in the marketplace. Finally, Peter Cannell, the Press's Director, deserves our thanks as well.

In something of a reversal of the usual process, *Spirit Capture* gave rise to an exhibition of the same name that will open at our George Gustav Heye Center in Manhattan in early 1999. Gratitude is in order to those who have worked so hard on the exhibition side of the equation. Again, we thank book contributors Tim Johnson, Rick Hill, and Natasha Bonilla Martinez for their inspired service as co-curators of the exhibition. Their vision and knowledge have enabled NMAI to gather and present significant new information on, and insights into, our unparalleled photo collection. In addition, Herman Viola, Curator Emeritus at the National Museum of Natural History, let us call upon his extensive knowledge of Native photography. The *Spirit Capture* exhibition would not have been possible without the assistance, contributions, recollections, and expertise of many individuals and Native communities across the continent, too numerous to list here. The knowledge and resources generously shared with us by so many people add considerably to the importance and educational value of the museum's holdings.

Major exhibitions such as *Spirit Capture* would not be possible without the contributions of many dedicated members of the NMAI staff. First off, Charlotte Heth, Assistant Director for Public Programs, deserves much credit for her creative oversight of our Exhibitions and Publications departments. The exhibition was created under the leadership and guidance of project director Jim Volkert, while exhibit developer Jim Rubinstein managed and coordinated all aspects of the project. Special thanks must be given to the staff of NMAI's Photo Archive— including Pamela Dewey, Janine Sarna Jones, Katherine Fogden, and Nema Magovern—for the extraordinary work they've done to support this project in countless ways. NMAI Curator Mary Jane Lenz, senior member of the staff headed so ably by Assistant Director for Cultural

Resources Bruce Bernstein, coordinated the selection and research for those museum objects that are included in the exhibition. John Colonghi, John Carlin, and the staff of our National Campaign Office were instrumental in securing resources to make this project possible.

Significant contributions in content development, research and scripting, artifact selection and preparation, media production, and exhibit design and installation were provided by staff from the museum's Community Services, Administration, Exhibitions, and Publications offices in Washington, D.C.; the NMAI Cultural Resources offices in New York and Washington; and the Film and Video Center, Exhibitions and Education departments, and Resource Center, all based in the George Gustav Heye Center in New York. For all their dedicated work, we are very thankful.

Finally, our gratitude goes to the Smithsonian Women's Committee, which awarded us a much-appreciated grant to support the processing of our photographic images.

W. RICHARD WEST, DIRECTOR
(Southern Cheyenne and member of the Cheyenne
and Arapaho Tribes of Oklahoma)

Introduction

Gazes Forward
from the Past

Tim Johnson

Even though it was more than thirty years ago, I clearly remember the last six-and-a-half miles my family would drive to my great-grandmother's homestead on the Six Nations Indian Reserve. I grew up within the relatively stable and secure environment of a suburb of Buffalo, New York, with paved and lighted streets, efficient new schools and grocery stores, doctors' and dentists' offices, and the reassuring, pungent odor of a nearby chemical plant. I always felt as if I were entering an alternate reality the instant our tires made contact with the gravel of Fourth Line Road.

The reserve was a world far different from that in which I formed my earliest impressions. It was neither better nor worse, but it presented contrasts that forever piqued my curiosity and shaped the perspectives of my thinking and, indeed, of the very direction of my life. I distinctly remember the smell of that gravel dust as our car kicked up a trail that floated in the air for minutes. I recall the sounds of the beetles and crickets on a homeland territory that was simply and quite affectionately referred to as "The Bush." The look and feel of my great-grandmother's house remain with me, a house that had no running water and no television set. The smell of the wood smoke that drifted from the stove she used to both cook her food and heat her home still lingers. And like indelible prints forever etched upon my mind, I remember the old photographs that hung on the west wall of her house.

The photographs were much like those proudly displayed by most families. Primarily portraits of the paternal side of my father's family, they included a studio portrait of great-grandfather Richard Johnson posing in his Canadian army uniform. He served as an army cook in World War I. To our family's disappointment, this photograph has since been lost, but its memory continues to fuel discussions about the conscription of Iroquois men into the Canadian and American armed forces.

2. Susan Jane Johnson, a Mohawk Wolf clanmother, with her son, Robert Harold Johnson. Six Nations Reserve, Ohsweken, Ontario, Canada. Courtesy of Tim Johnson.

3. Susan Jane and Richard Johnson. Six Nations Reserve, Ohsweken, Ontario, Canada. Courtesy of Tim Johnson.

In a matrilineal Iroquois social system, however, it was my great-grandmother Susan Jane Johnson (fig. 2) who dominated life and lore at the homestead. I greatly enjoy looking at the portrait of her and her son, my grandfather Robert Harold Johnson. Matriarch Susan was more than ninety years old when my family took those long drives to visit her on weekends. I still think of her as a cautiously moving elder (fig. 3), not as the young, vibrant woman who lived off the land. Although she was a traditional clanmother of the Mohawk Bear Clan, she was also a devout Anglican who, for sixty-seven years, played the pump organ for St. John's Church on the corner of Fifth Line and Tuscarora Roads on the reserve. Her ability to straddle both the traditional Iroquois culture and the Christian faith indicates one of several seeming contradictions, accommodations, or simple realities that still prevail in Native communities today.

Photographs of my father's maternal side of the family also influenced the general Indian education I received while growing up. Of particular relevance were images of my grandmother Florence Hill and her three sisters, all of whom had moved to Hamilton, Ontario, to live. Like my great-grandmother Susan, they were born in tiny "settlement" log cabins on the reserve. I prize with particular affection those photographs and news clippings of my great-uncle Emerson Hill, Shar-eh-ho-wah-neh, a Wolf Clan Mohawk chief of the Iroquois Confederacy. Uncle Emerson was a hardworking and hard-living ironworker who devoted most of his free time to his duties as a traditional chief—a position without pay or, usually, recognition.

Since contact was first made with Europeans and through the historical developments of nation states in North America, a traditional core of Iroquois leaders has maintained its own national structures and identities, and even when divided, has sustained its cultural and political savvy with a sense of common purpose.[1] Emerson Hill was no different, and my family is fortunate that a few of our photographs show him upholding his responsibilities as tribal leader. One such image documents his attendance at a meeting with government officials in Washington, D.C., on 20 July 1954, at which a delegation from the Six Nations Iroquois Confederacy explained the meaning of various wampum belts and the international agreements they symbolized (fig. 4). This family photograph represents an ongoing process by which traditional Indian leadership in the Americas continues to inform mainstream political figures about established government-to-government relations. It is an honor for our family to possess such an image.

Some of my great-uncle Emerson's spirit comes to life in a yellowed, tattered news clipping. While traveling through the United Kingdom after a lecture tour in Sweden in 1970, he presented an Iroquois passport for immigration officials to inspect.

> Home Secretary Reginald Maudling was asked yesterday how an Iroquois chief from Ontario managed to enter Britain on documents drawn up by himself and other tribal leaders. . . .
>
> The question was occasioned by the arrival at London's Heathrow Airport recently of Iroquois chief Emerson Hill of Oshweken [sic]. Mr. Hill was returning to Canada from a lecture tour of Sweden, where he spoke on Iroquois "independence."

4. Six Nations Iroquois Confederacy delegation to Washington, D.C., 20 July 1954. P26510

Lawyer Martin Lowe said he represented Mr. Hill after the 60-year-old chief decided to stop over in Britain but refused to produce a Canadian passport when asked by immigration officials. . . .

Mr. Hill especially reveled in telling the immigration men that no one asked their ancestors for passports when they landed in Canada for the first time, and Mr. Lowe added: "It was all done as a matter of principle as far as he (Hill) was concerned and he went home happily the following Monday."[2]

While this particular news story centered on one casual confrontation at a border post in England, the freedom to cross borders and the right to maintain one's distinct national identity have been the basis of Iroquois and other Indian positions for hundreds of years. My first understandings of this issue began with a simple photograph, a "head shot" of my uncle at the top of that news column. From a small collection of family photographs I learned at an early age that life can be highly complex and challenging (fig. 5).

In my mainstream world, life and future seemed not guaranteed but much more certain and better defined: go to school, do your homework, say your prayers, abide by the law, pledge allegiance to God and country, and work hard to achieve professional and material objectives. I struggled desperately to fit snugly into that pattern, but from my earliest conscious days I could

5. (above left) Delegation crossing the international bridge at Niagara Falls, at the first annual celebration of border-crossing privileges to all Indians, 14 July 1928. Presented by Clinton Rickard, Chief, Beaver Clan, Tuscarora Reservation, New York. P14081

6. (above right) Chief Two Leggings (Absaroke [Crow]) before leading a parade, ca. 1919. Photo by Willem Wildschut. N31070

7. (below left) Kwakiutl women at Christian service. Vancouver Island, British Columbia, Canada. N36096 (P7870)

8. Apache girls at the Carlisle Indian School. Carlisle, Pennsylvania. Photo by John N. Choate. P6940

9. Runaway Wyandot girls being returned to boarding school, 1901. Col. Frank C. Churchill Collection. N27364

10. Dakota Indians receiving rations, 1908. Fort Peck, Montana. Photo by Col. Frank C. Churchill. Col. Frank C. Churchill Collection. N27587

11. Group portrait of Indian police (possibly Navajo), ca. 1900. Photo by Sumner Matteson. P23984

never adequately reconcile the cultural duality of my existence after I was first enlightened by those family photos. I went to school but questioned incessantly the history I was taught. I went to church but at first opportunity rejected identification with its institutional structures and methods. I railed against the powerful force of law that marched mightily over Indian lands, rights, and freedoms. At school I would stand but could not voice allegiance to the flag. And I worked hard throughout my life, perhaps all too successfully, not to build a career or to accumulate possessions, but to educate and advocate on behalf of indigenous peoples within this hemisphere and around the world. I have lived largely with an Indian spirit in a non-Indian environment (figs. 5, 6, 7, 8; see fig. 132).

In my Indian world, life and future are more tenuous, not necessarily in a personal way, but in a community way (figs. 9–11). In many cases the issues our community faces are complex to the point of division and paralysis. It is here, amid a culture rich in environmental ethics and agricultural values, that most families no longer work the land. It is here where four traditional longhouses and many more churches service a variety of religious organizations and denominations. It is here where social issues are of great concern. Yet it is also here where personal freedoms remain liberal and broad in scope, and where, for all their differences, people remain attached to a land base upon which they still share a core indigenous identity. And it is here where fortunate elders, adults, and children still soothe the earth with the rhythms of this land's original languages.

How did it get this way? How have so many institutional changes forged such a multicultural reality from a once-homogenous people? To varying degrees these questions apply to Indian communities throughout the Western Hemisphere. Many of the answers can be found in the personal collections of photographs held by Indian families and in the archives of great educational institutions, such as the National Museum of the American Indian. Like gazes forward from the past, the images of our ancestors speak volumes—but only if we are prepared to see clearly and to listen amid the silence.

The photographic archive of the National Museum of the American Indian (NMAI) of the Smithsonian Institution holds approximately 90,000 images, including 47,000 negatives, 30,000 vintage prints, and 13,500 transparencies, lantern slides, and glass plate negatives. It is considered one of the world's most significant collections of images that document Native American peoples of the Western Hemisphere.[3] While the collection ranges from mid-nineteenth-century daguerreotypes to color slides that record contemporary Native American artists and events, its reputation is built upon field photography from the early twentieth century. Given the vastness of the museum's archive, this book can merely serve as an introduction to a largely unexplored world.

George Gustav Heye (fig. 12), founder of the Museum of the American Indian, Heye Foundation (which is now incorporated into the NMAI), collected not only material objects made by Native Americans but also photographs that documented the artifacts, dress, daily habits, and ceremonial life of the peoples he encountered. From his earliest endeavors, Heye considered photography to be an important tool for collecting information about the Indian cultures that many Americans then thought were becoming obscured by new and more dominant political, social, and spiritual institutions.[4] Over time the archive grew as Heye solicited and purchased images from photographers, anthropologists (fig. 13), and private collectors. He procured ever older images and greatly expanded the breadth of the collection both in terms of its time span and its geographic coverage, an immense range covering hundreds of Indian nations extending from the Arctic (fig. 14) to Tierra del Fuego (fig. 15).

A formal photography department was established at Heye's museum in 1955, and during the 1960s, photographer Carmelo Guadagno performed significant preservation and cataloguing programs. In the 1980s, under the direction of then Assistant Curator of Photography Natasha Bonilla [Martinez], the museum sought to increase the collection's public exposure by renewing its efforts to protect and preserve its vast photographic resources and to increase public access to the collection.

A mandate of Heye's museum—to ensure public access—continues under NMAI's current stewardship. In recent years public interest in Native American peoples has increased tremendously, as is evident by the growing numbers of publications about Natives and the

12. George Gustav Heye, ca. 1915. Nacochee Mound, Georgia. N34267

13. Shuar on the trail with Victor Wolfgang von Hagen on an expedition, ca. 1935. Oriente, Ecuador. N36829

14. Bering Strait Eskimo (Inuit) hunters, ca. 1908–15. Alaska. Lomen Brothers Studio, Nome, Alaska. N35421

15. Ona couple, Tierra del Fuego.

Photo by E.L. Bridges. N20235

production of motion pictures, made-for-television movies, and documentaries. Researchers and publishers request hundreds of photographs from the archive each year. Quite likely most Americans have seen photographs from the collection, whether in history books or on the television set. The impact these images have had on public perceptions of Native peoples is substantial and profound. As "couriers" of information, these photos have helped shape a nation's understanding of Indian life for nearly one hundred years.

Through this book we hope to heighten public awareness not only of the archive's vast holdings but also of the depth and breadth of the Native American experience. Several noted authorities on photography, Indian history, and the NMAI's photo archive have lent their personal and professional expertise to this project.

From her unique perspective as former assistant curator of the photography department at the Museum of the American Indian, Heye Foundation, Natasha Bonilla Martinez discusses the life of George Gustav Heye and the development of his outstanding collection of Indian artifacts and photographs. She also delves into four collections acquired by Heye and one expedition he sponsored in his pursuit of forming a comprehensive representation of Native American culture in the Western Hemisphere. Her section on the Hendricks-Hodge Expedition was co-authored with Rose Wyaco, a Zuni tribal member. Ms. Martinez now lives in San Marcos, California, and is sole proprietor of Cultura Works. Additional insights into the history and holdings of the NMAI's wide-ranging photography archive are provided by Pamela Dewey, head of the archive, and Laura Nash, formerly the museum's curatorial assistant of photography.

Nigel H. Russell, curator of The Spira Collection in New York City, contributes a historical overview of the evolution of photography and its use to document Native Americans. He emphasizes the technological innovations that affected the way photographs were taken and presented from the mid nineteenth century to the present day.

Richard W. Hill, Sr. (Tuscarora), assistant professor of American Studies at the State University of New York at Buffalo, explores the development and perpetuation of stereotypical images of Native Americans in fine art and photography. Hill, who has organized dozens of art and museum exhibitions, has spent a lifetime researching and speaking on this subject.

Linda Poolaw brings a personal view to these photographs, one based on her life as a Kiowa–Delaware Indian and her memories of her father, the photographer Horace Poolaw, whose works complement her essay. Her concern for the future of Indians has expanded to

16. Portrait of Chief Joseph
(Wallowa Band of the Nez Percé),
1897. Photo by Wells M. Sawyer.
Gen. Nelson A. Miles Collection.

P7010

include her investigation into the causes of heart disease among Indians, which is the focus of her work at the Anadarko Indian Health Clinic for the University of Oklahoma Health Sciences Center. Together, these writers and scholars enable us to trace the development of photography and the growth of the NMAI, as well as to participate in the continuing interpretation and reevaluation of Indian history.

In addition to the contributions of these authors, several photographers were commissioned to explore and document continuing aspects of contemporary Native life, culture, and community. Among them was Janine Sarna Jones, a staff photographer at the NMAI. Her photographs of descendants of Indian subjects found in the museum's archive form a visually engaging bridge between the past and the present.

Larry McNeil, a studio and editorial photographer based in Santa Fe, New Mexico, documented the working and artistic life of Alaska Indians. He is currently president of the Native Indian Inuit Photographer's Association.

A member of the Turtle Mountain Chippewa in North Dakota, Dorothy Grandbois confronted her own childhood memories by photographing an Indian boarding school. She was sent from home at age five to attend Catholic and government boarding schools. The experience left an indelible impression on her life and work, which is evident in her writings and award-winning photographs.

Larry Gus, a Native freelance editorial and studio photographer based in Los Angeles, contributed images of Indian casino gaming, while Katherine Fogden, a photographer with the NMAI, returned to her home community of Akwesasne (Where the Partridge Drums) to record the diverse spiritual traditions of her Mohawk people.

Researchers and curators who have extensively studied the archive express a common sentiment: the same images have been ordered and repeatedly used by various media over the years. Many of us have seen the more dramatic pictures of American Indians and their history. How can we not admire the dignified countenance of Heinmot Toolalakeet (In-mut-too-yah-lat-lat), Nez Percé Chief Joseph (fig. 16), whose civil leadership and impassioned oratory established a legacy of strength and perseverance for Indian people under the most trying of circumstances?

17. Portrait of Goyathlay
(Geronimo), Chiricahua Apache.
Photo probably by Frank A.
Rinehart. P17811

It is cold and we have no blankets. The little children are freezing to death. My people, some of them, have run away to the hills, and have no blankets, no food; no one knows where they are—perhaps freezing to death. I want to have time to look for my children and see how many of them I can find. Maybe I shall find them among the dead. From where the sun now stands I will fight no more forever.[5]

Even after his surrender speech in 1877, following a gallant flight evading American armies for more than a thousand miles, Chief Joseph continued to advocate the cause of his people. In those old photos his gaze projects forward in time. His problems seem no less different than those encountered in many Native communities today, and his moral leadership still provides a framework for his descendants.

Our fathers gave us many laws, which they had learned from their fathers. These laws were good. They told us to treat all men as they treated us; that we should never be the first to break a bargain; that it was a disgrace to tell a lie; that we should speak only the truth; that it was a shame for one man to take from another his wife, or his property without paying for it. We were taught to believe that the Great Spirit sees and hears everything, and that he never forgets; that hereafter he will give every man a spirit home according to his deserts; if he has been a good man, he will have a good home; if he has been a bad man he will have a bad home. This I believe, and all my people believe the same.[6]

Perhaps no Indian leader has been more vilified or stereotyped than Goyathlay (One Who Yawns; Geronimo). His image (fig. 17), taken at different times throughout his life and now stored in the photographic archive, records the transitions of an embattled defender of Indian life and lands. After the slaughter of his mother, his wife Alope, and their three children by Mexican troops in 1858, he spent years engaged in armed conflicts. His strident oratory presented an original Apache point of view. Whether on the battlefield or in the community, his valiant attempts to maintain his people's freedoms and values were admirable.

This image of an armed killer, kneeling with rifle in hand (see fig. 88), may yet prevail in popular impressions, yet many of us know this man intimately. In my own community I have gazed into the eyes of several contemporary versions of him. Goyathlay's work in opposing the planned dismantling of the Apache culture filled a void at a time when other leaders, such as the Chiricahua chief Cochise, had died, had lost the will to define their own destiny, or had simply acquiesced in the face of insurmountable odds.[7]

From the perspective of Native Americans, there exists perhaps no more striking symbol of the route of American expansion than the Wounded Knee massacre of 29 December 1890. A few images in the NMAI collection depict events before and after that tragic incident (figs. 18, 19). Beyond even the horror of the killings, it is the context of the event that yields the epic despair of a people at the end of any options they had envisioned for a self-determined future.

Famous images abound in this massive photographic archive, but the strength, indeed the real spirit of the collection, resides in what most people rarely glimpse. Within the NMAI photographic archive thousands of images subtly communicate an American history that

18. (above) Big Foot's (Minneconjou Lakota) band at a Grass Dance on the Cheyenne River, South Dakota, 9 August 1890. Most of the band was killed at Wounded Knee. N39356 (P7000)

19. *Burial of the Dead at the Battle of Wounded Knee, South Dakota, 1891.* Photo by George R. Trager. N37900

20. Klamath, Modoc, Paiute, and Pit River Indians signing declaration of allegiance to the United States, 1913. Klamath Falls, Oregon. Wanamaker Expedition. Photo by Joseph Dixon. N36063

21. Portrait of Stephen Pharoah (Montauk), 1867. Long Island, New York. N34834

presents a fearful and bewildering saga of conversion and transition felt by Native American peoples who, even today, are still in the process of adjustment (fig. 20).

Tekamthi (Shooting Star; Tecumseh) of the Shawnee once said, "Where today are the Pequot? Where are the Narraganset, the Mohican, the Pokanoket, and many other once powerful tribes of our people? They have vanished before the avarice and the oppression of the White Man, as snow before a summer sun."[8] It is true that the enormous burden of survival thrust upon Native peoples during the course of European expansion led many, white and Indian alike, to believe that Indians would vanish from the land. In some cases they have, and we find memory of their faces only in the museum's archive—but many Indian nations also survived (fig. 21). The Mashantucket Pequot have reemerged from obscurity to reclaim their heritage and ascend to economic power in the very lands where they once had seemingly disappeared.

The essence of the NMAI photo archive, and therefore of this book, is that most of the images in the collection reveal Indian peoples experiencing times of dramatic change in their lives—times when they did not have a clear sense of a sustainable future. From the image of a delegation crossing the international bridge at Niagara Falls, to Apache girls at the Carlisle Indian School, to the Seminole woman sewing in Florida, to the Yaqui man in Sonora, Mexico, to the Assiniboine women on horseback near Edmonton, Alberta, and to many other images of

Native peoples and communities across the hemisphere, the photographic archive is a collective witness to Indian transitions.

Five years ago I spent four months combing through the collection. The thousands of faces I viewed while conducting my research stayed with me, permeating my soul. Many, if not all, of these Indians lived through challenging times, and I sensed their bewilderment, wonder, and expectation. There is sadness in those old faces, but also glints and glimmers of hope and profound reflections of humanity. I feel honored to have met so many Indian relatives this way. My curiosity, I imagine, was not unlike that of the many non-Native photographers whose own personal explorations added to their quest for knowledge and adventure.

On horse-drawn wagons, trains, and automobiles, photographers ventured throughout the Western Hemisphere in search of Native peoples. They wanted to document the origins of objects and artifacts they collected, to capture historical moments, to record for posterity the faces of Indian leaders, men, women, and children. Some were formally educated and used photography as a tool to support their intellectual inquiries. Others were studio photographers who sold their services and images, and still others were simply curious hobbyists. Together, their efforts of mixed intentions and varied technical and aesthetic skills have come to form this substantial body of work, the photographic archive of the National Museum of the American Indian.

Works taken by more than ninety photographers and expedition groups are housed in the collection. Their assembly all began with George Gustav Heye's practice of using photography to record excavations, artifacts, landscapes, and Indians. To ensure that the objects collected would retain their significance, Heye had the artifacts photographed *in situ* to keep their function and meaning intact. Many images do not name the persons who wear the articles of clothing or use the very objects that Heye collected for his museum. Catalogue numbers of the objects shown are listed on many photographs, but the identities of the Native peoples remain a mystery.

Among the many ethnographers, archaeologists, and collectors who documented their work for the museum are Alanson Buck Skinner, Edward H. Davis, George Pepper, A. H. Verrill, and Dr. Mark Raymond Harrington. Others known for their field photography include Willem Wildschut, Frederick Johnson, and Dr. Frank G. Speck. The collection is also distinguished for the historical portraits and studies by photographers such as Edward Sheriff Curtis, John Hillers, Timothy H. O'Sullivan, and William Henry Jackson.

It is important, when viewing these images, to accommodate the context of the historical development of photography and the historical development of events among Native Americans. Most of the images of Indian subjects in the NMAI collection were taken by non-Native photographers. The world realities on which both photographers and subjects based their actions could hardly have been more distant. Hulleah J. Tsinhnahjinnie chronicles these parallel developments as follows:

1830–1850. Andrew Jackson initiated the Removal Act. All tribes east of the Mississippi were to be relocated west (the Cherokee Trail of Tears, Choctaw removal, Creek removal, etc.) [see figs. 22, 23].

22. Cherokee girl, 1899. Tahlequah, Oklahoma. Col. Frank C. Churchill Collection. N27301

Meanwhile Niepce and Daguerre were collaborating on the development of photography, and when the process was presented to the world, portraits were being taken everywhere.

1850–1870. The carte-de-visite became the rage, stereoscopic photography was patented, cameras were constantly being improved. Meanwhile reservations had been established, and northern tribes were now in the way of American settlers. The Yakimas, Cayuses, Wallawallas, Spokanes, Palouses, and Coeur d'Alenes were moved to reservations. The Navajos were forced on the long walk to Fort

Sumner, New Mexico; smallpox wiped out two-thirds of the already dwindling population of the Northwest Coast tribes.

1870–1900. Faster plates were available, Eadweard Muybridge photographed a horse in mid gallop close to 1/500th of a second. Lt. Col. George Custer and his men met the Sioux at Little Bighorn. Chief Joseph led his people north to Canada and was stopped less than thirty miles from the border.

The Dawes Act. The Oklahoma land rush. Eastman produced the Kodak—"you press the button, we do the rest." Photography was now available to the amateur masses, but Native interest was in the power of the Ghost Dance, a return to the way it was before the white man. Even though in 1890 the Kodak camera was available in seven different designs, not one photograph of the Wounded Knee massacre is from the Native point of view. Stieglitz photographed lower Manhattan, Steichen bought his first camera, and Native people dealt with forced assimilation, land allotment procedures, and religious persecution.

1900–1939. The Brownie camera was introduced and marketed to children, and the quick-focus Kodak and the Leica appeared. Meanwhile oil was discovered on Native lands in Oklahoma, and oil-rich Natives were murdered or declared incompetent. Native people dealt with the Indian Reorganization Act, the structuring of tribal governments, establishing control of resources, and the beginning of the termination period.[9]

Questions linger about the impact of the camera's intrusion into traditional community life (figs. 24–26). Some Native peoples avoided the camera, fearing that it might capture their spirits or provoke illnesses.[10] At other times photographers who did not respect tribal customs would photograph events, sacred sites, or ceremonies that were not normally open for public documentation. George Wharton James explained how he photographed an otherwise forbidden scene.

23. Portrait of David Owl (Cherokee) with his grandson, 1908. Col. Frank C. Churchill Collection. N23380

It was with trepidation I dared to take my camera into the mystic depths of the Antelope Kiva. I had guessed at focus for the altar, and when I placed the camera against the wall, pointed toward the sacred place, the Antelope priests bid me remove it immediately. I begged to have it remain so long as I stayed, but was compelled to promise I would not place my head under the black cloth and look at the altar. This I readily promised, but at the first opportunity when no one was between the lens and the altar, I quietly removed the cap from the lens, marched away and sat down with one of the priests, while the dim light performed its wonderful work on the sensitive plate. A fine photograph was the result.[11]

Similar actions by photographers over the years have caused Indian peoples to become cautious when cameras appear near their family spaces and places of worship. Museums such as

24. (above left) Catawba man and boy hunting with a blowgun, 1922. South Carolina. Photo by Frank G. Speck. N12398

25. (above right) Seminole family, ca. 1920. N37235

26. View of Zuni (the Paquin family?) "waffle" gardens, 1919. New Mexico. Photo by Frederick Webb Hodge or Jesse L. Nusbaum. Hendricks-Hodge Expedition. P11433

the NMAI have become more accommodating to the values of those peoples and cultures they document and represent. According to Willow Roberts Powers and Richard W. Hill, Sr., authors of *Images Across Boundaries,* photographic images of American Indians fall into two major categories: sacred and secular. They stress that photographs of ritual objects and altars, religious dances, and an array of related subjects specific to tribal traditional practices are sacred images.[12]

Powers and Hill are not alone in their contention that many photographs have indeed been obtained without permission, and such images carry knowledge that should not be shared with the uninitiated. Publishing such images would "trespass" on the delicate philosophical and spiritual balances of long-established community ethics. Out of respect for this concept, no ceremonial images are reproduced in this book. The collection, however, remains open and available for tribal representatives who wish to view photographs that may have been taken of sacred objects, acts, and sites as defined by the Native peoples themselves. To do otherwise would destroy opportunities for museum staff members to engage in a productive dialogue with their constituencies and to exchange information and knowledge.

Being the only Indian member of the photographic staff when I was working as a news photographer for the *Niagara Gazette* in 1987, I was not particularly surprised when I was approached by the paper's archivist one day. He presented me with a box of news photographs of Indians taken by several different photographers over the years. The archivist was cleaning out his files and asked me if I wanted the images. Most of them depicted people and events of the Tuscarora Indian Nation, the only Native community within the *Gazette*'s constituency.

Inside the box were neatly stacked images of a Tuscarora picnic, of elders, chiefs, and clanmothers, and of the armed struggles with the New York State Power Authority in 1957, when a large portion of the reservation was confiscated to construct a reservoir. Pictured at the height of their powers were Chief Clinton Rickard, Wallace "Mad Bear" Anderson with his group of community activists, and Harry "Jiggy" Hill leading the annual border-crossing parade across the Whirlpool Bridge in Niagara Falls. These were clearly important documents of Tuscarora Indian life extending from the early 1950s to the 1970s.

What also struck me about many of the images was the way they looked. Of course, they all had that sort of "news style" aesthetic of those times, yet some of the photos were bizarre and seemingly out of context. I remember an image taken at the Tuscarora picnic of two elders in Indian dress holding ears of corn up to the sky in an offering of prayer. I saw images from the 1960s of Indian children sitting in trees and pretending to hunt with little bows and arrows. One photograph showed an Indian hatchet thrower. Another was a close-up portrait of an Indian in feathers eating a hot dog. In a third an Indian looked quizzically at a radio in the 1970s. Just where did these photographers get their ideas of Indian life? And why did the Indians so graciously play along?

These questions and their difficult answers are part of an ongoing quest to understand the relationship that has evolved largely between non-Indians as photographers and Indians as subjects.

KEOKUK, OR THE WATCHFUL FOX.   SAC & FOX

27. Kicking Bear (Minneconjou Lakota), 1896, a warrior and leader in the Ghost Dance movement. Photo by William Dinwiddie. P22431

28. Keokuk (Watchful Fox, or One Who Moves About Alert), a Sac and Fox war chief, 1847. Daguerreotype by Thomas M. Easterly, St. Louis. Jackson Catalogue 672. P2030

This complex relationship has been influenced by many factors. When I looked at those *Niagara Gazette* photos I was also compelled to ask why, perhaps more than with any other cultural and racial group in America, do Indians remain so fixed in seemingly surrealistic imagery?

The NMAI Photo Archive contains thousands of images that reveal the photographers' particular points of view. Both images and archive have served to define attitudes toward Indians over the decades. While ethnic and cultural stereotyping remains a burning issue, a symbiotic relationship also exists that begs examination. The Tuscaroras in those *Gazette* photos were willing players, participants in the development of their own imagery. Although it was not always the case, Indians have, to a certain degree, bought into the process. Contemporary Indian powwows, managed and promoted by Indians themselves, cater to prevailing images and are among the most photographed events in the country.

My great-grandmother Susan Johnson was an amazing woman. Upon intellectual reflection she can be seen as a living example of contradictions born out of changing times. Such

29. (above left) Shuar (?) man.
Mato Grosso, Brazil. Photo
possibly by W. Garbe. N34456

30. (above right) Two women.
N36053

31. Blood medicine woman, ca. 1900.
Calgary, Alberta, Canada. Photo by
Harry Pollard. N36878 (P13227)

contradictions are evident in every Native community affected by the confusing array of institutions that teach different ways of doing things. Since 1492 virtually everything Indians encountered has been different: the ways of living off the land, learning, dressing, and preparing food. The ways of speaking, governing, and conducting family relationships have been different. Indeed, the very ways of considering concepts through new languages have been different.

These differences have been expressed repeatedly in Native American testimony through the ages. On the use of written words, Sac and Fox war chief Ma-ka-tai-me-she-kia-kiak (Black Hawk) stated in 1834, "Here for the first time, I touched the goose quill to the treaty, not knowing, however, that, by that act, I consented to give away my village. Had that been explained to me, I should have opposed it, and never would have signed their treaty, as my recent conduct will clearly prove. What do we know of the manner of the laws and customs of the white people?"[13] In 1871, Chiricahua chief Cochise observed on religion, "Tell me, if Virgin Mary has walked throughout all the land, why has she never entered the wigwam of the Apache? Why have we never seen or heard her?"[14]

It is here, within this realm of sweeping social and cultural change, that we encounter the "spirit" of the NMAI's photographic archive. Virtually every image in the collection attests to this process of change, for the camera itself was a recorder of differences. Set against European-based cultural realities, these thousands of images stand as documents of difference (figs. 27–31). The histories, outcomes, and continuing issues of the Indian-European encounter are still being played out and are still very much in debate. These photographs indeed "capture" the origins of much of the debate, the stark impact of the encounter, and the "spirit" or will of Indian peoples to continue to be who they are as they adjust to their changing realities. In many ways it is a painful, heartbreaking visual journey. In other ways, it is a story of redemption, in which you can almost smell the smoked leather in the tipi, hear the melodic and rhythmic voices of the elders sharing the old stories, or taste the caribou meat cooked in a northern Cree camp tent. These surviving visual threads of Indian cultural identity are the synapses that connect us all to the Native spirit of the Western Hemisphere. That this spirit has been "captured" at all, in the tens of thousands of images in the NMAI Photo Archive, is remarkable. It requires our best intellectual and emotional impulses to appreciate and understand the lives and histories of the original peoples and cultures of the Americas. The powerful images and words in this book will assist all of us to arrive at a better understanding of the resonance of this cultural encounter and change as it has been recorded during the past 150 splendid years of photography.

*Photographs by
Janine Sarna Jones*

During my work in the NMAI Photo Archive, I have often considered the notion that many of the museum's photographs are missing from the family photo albums of thousands of Native families. There are children in these photographs who probably grew to have their own children, grandchildren, and great-grandchildren long before I began working with their images. How many of these children's children know of their connection to these photographs? How many are aware that a part of themselves—their ancestry—has been archived?

I have been fortunate to witness Native visitors recognize family, identify people, and connect themselves to images in the collection. The Family Photos Project came out of a desire to share these connections with others, and to show that these photographs are of individuals who are still with us—in their progeny and in their traditions. –J.S.J.

32. Willie Seaweed, a Kwakiutl chief, 1951. Blunden Harbor, British Columbia, Canada. The hat in this photograph is now in the NMAI collection (23.8252). Photo by William R. Heick. N41440 (P19648)

33. Henry Seaweed, grandson of Willie Seaweed, November 1996. Vancouver, British Columbia, Canada. Photo by Janine Sarna Jones. P26535

Henry Seaweed is the grandson of distinguished Southern Kwakiutl carver, Chief Willie Seaweed. Henry's childhood was spent in Blunden Harbor, British Columbia, learning Kwakwala songs and dances from his grandfather, chief of the Nakwaxda'xw tribe. A retired Canadian postal worker, Henry is an accomplished Kwakiutl dancer and spends a great part of his time traveling and performing.

34. From left: Frank Cornplanter, Bacon Rind, and Henry Red Eagle (Osage), 1903. Pawhuska, Oklahoma. Col. Frank C. Churchill Collection. N27177

35. Nema (right) and Erin Magovern, great-great-granddaughter and great-great-great-granddaughter of Henry Red Eagle, November 1996. West Long Branch, New Jersey. Photo by Janine Sarna Jones. P26536

36. Albert Henry (Choctaw), 1908. Mississippi. Photo by Mark R. Harrington. N2676

37. Nelson Henry, grandnephew of Albert Henry, September 1996. Philadelphia, Mississippi. Photo by Janine Sarna Jones. P26537

Nelson Henry is a grandnephew of Albert Henry, and currently works for the Mississippi Band of Choctaw Indians. Nelson attended the University of Missouri while working for the forestry division near St. Louis. Nineteen years ago, Nelson returned to Mississippi to work for his tribe and is now a supervisor for the tribe's Department of Agriculture and Rural Development.

Related to Indian leaders through her mother and to U. S. Marshalls through her father, Nema Magovern grew up in Hominy, Oklahoma. She is a great-great-granddaugther of Henry Red Eagle, an Osage medicine man, and a great-grandniece of Bacon Rind, an Osage chief. Nema worked in the fashion industry for 30 years prior to coming to work at NMAI's Photo Archive. Nema's daughter Erin has also worked in the fashion industry and is currently pursuing a degree in marketing at Monmouth College. Each June, Nema and Erin return to Oklahoma for the annual Osage ceremonial dances. Nema learned the value of practicing Osage traditions from her mother's family and says that maintaining a traditional life "gave me extra confidence, and I certainly know it gives my daughter that."

1. An Indian Americas

NMAI Photographic Archive Documents Indian Peoples of the Western Hemisphere

Natasha Bonilla Martinez

Ever since the earliest European chronicles described the exploration of the New World, Europeans and later Euroamericans have been fascinated with images of the indigenous people of the Americas. Like many others, artists commonly depicted Indians by combining mythic and stereotypic elements with observations drawn from life. From their earliest appearance, artists' drawings, woodcuts, and lithographs of Indian subjects reflected European preoccupations as much as any objective representation of Native reality. When photography was invented more than three centuries after those initial encounters, its possibilities provided new and exciting methods to depict Native peoples. The first known photograph of a Native American was made in Great Britain around 1845.[1] By the 1850s scores of Indian leaders traveled to Washington, D.C., to negotiate treaties with the federal government and to sit for formal delegation portraits. After the Civil War, photographers on government-sponsored expeditions began to create a visual record of the American Indian in the West. The rest, we can say, is photographic history.

The vast photographic collection at the National Museum of the American Indian (NMAI) reflects the monumental—and ultimately unfathomable—desire of George Gustav Heye to possess as many objects as possible made by and representing the Indians of the Americas. Beginning with an incidental purchase of a single hide shirt in 1897, Heye amassed a collection of more than one million objects by the time of his death in 1957. It stands out as the largest and most comprehensive collection of its kind ever created. The assembled masterworks and everyday objects represent nearly every tribe and most aspects of the pre-Columbian and historical eras (fig. 38). Although he died more than forty years ago, Heye's vision in many ways still defines the collections and their organization.

The NMAI's photographic collection contains approximately 90,000 images of men, women, children, fathers, mothers, grandparents, siblings, aunts, uncles, and cousins participating in

38. Blood, Piegan, and Sarsi encampment, ca. 1900. Near Gleichen, Alberta, Canada. N41393 (P20874)

39. Plains Cree basketmaker, ca.
1920. Prince Albert National Park,
Saskatchewan, Canada. N36877

40. Portrait of an Apache man, 1884.
Photo by G. Ben Wittick or A.
Frank Randall. N36018

celebrations, ceremonies, historic events, and everyday life (fig. 39). Unlike the artifacts that represent material products created directly by Native hands, these photographs are at once more intimate and potentially less personal. They record the lives of Native people, yet the moments depicted may be subtly distorted or filtered by the perspectives and views of the photographers whose intentions and ideologies may be more ambiguous and difficult to determine.

Today, photographs of Native Americans, some taken as many as 150 years ago, are startling in their beauty and ambiguity (fig. 40). Questions arise concerning the interplay of the camera's presumed capability to represent "objective" reality and the photographer's personal interpretation and vision of the subject. Is this the singular view of an anthropologist, a tourist, an artist, or a government official—or a little of each? What visual and ideological issues do these images reflect? More than 150 years after the invention of the medium, we can say that photography is not a neutral science or art, but we still lack the basic criteria to analyze image content.

The majority of the photographs in this collection were created before 1950, in an era of global colonialization and political domination that then, as now, largely denied Indians control over their lives, much less the process by which their images were recorded (figs. 41, 42). In turn,

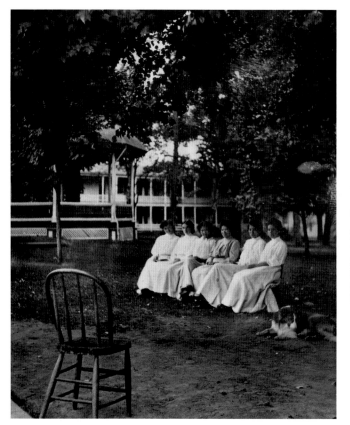

41. Women seated in front of
Carlisle Indian School. Carlisle,
Pennsylvania. N37601 [P618]

42. Baffin Island Eskimos (Inuit) in
the church at Lake Harbor, 1911.
Northwest Territories, Canada.
Photo by Robert Flaherty. P7725

the authority of those photographers, whether anthropologists, government agents, or tourists, to define those representations was not questioned.[2]

This narrative describes how the collection was assembled, and it presents some of the photographers' ideological and aesthetic concerns. It tells the story of how the collection came to embody many perspectives, beginning with Heye's vision as the institution's leader. The singular commonality of all the images is their collective concern to document the lives of Indian peoples in their Americas.

THE EARLY YEARS

From the beginning Heye's interest in photography was secondary. He did not collect photographs from any inherent interest in photography, but because the images represented Indians, and photography was key to anthropological documentation. In his early years of collecting, Heye sought to associate himself with the credibility of the anthropological endeavor.

Heye, the son of naturalized German oil entrepreneur Carl Friederich Gustav Heye, was born in 1874 and grew up in the exclusive Murray Hill area of New York City. He was educated at private schools and regularly traveled with his family to Europe, where he may have encountered

the German enthusiasm for Indian culture that was exemplified in the romantic novels of German author Karl May.[3]

The future collector came of age in an era when the Indian Wars were just coming to a close and the West was secured for expansion. In public venues, such as the 1876 Centennial Exhibition in Philadelphia and the 1893 Columbian Exposition in Chicago, "Indians were exhibited regularly as examples of America's past, or of primitive types in a great evolutionary chain of human progress," thereby establishing the accomplishments of progress in the nation and substantiating concepts of "Indian primitiveness and white superiority."[4] In museums, Indians and their artifacts not only were exhibited as scientific curiosities but also were integrated into similar evolutionary schemes that celebrated Europe's "triumphant present" over the earlier phases of mankind represented by Indians.[5]

In 1897 Heye, a recent graduate from the School of Mines at Columbia University with a degree in electrical engineering, traveled to Kingman, Arizona, to supervise a railway project. There the twenty-three-year-old Heye encountered Navajo laborers and purchased his first Indian souvenir, a leather shirt. Heye later said,

> I became interested in aboriginal customs, and acquired other objects as opportunity afforded, sending them back from time to time to my home at 11 East 48th Street. In fact, I spent more time collecting Navaho costume pieces and trinkets than I did superintending roadbeds. That shirt was the start of my collection. Naturally, when I had the shirt I wanted a rattle and moccasins. And then the collecting bug seized me and I was lost.

44. Maya (?) women making bread, 1900. Palenque, Chiapas, Mexico. Photo by Marshall H. Saville. N37556

When I returned to New York after about ten months in Arizona, I found quite an accumulation of articles. These I placed about my room and I began to read rather intensely on the subject of Indians.[6]

Heye accompanied Joseph Keppler, a political cartoonist at *Puck* magazine, on a visit to the Seneca and Cattaraugus Reservations in upstate New York in 1899. Keppler had become interested in the Iroquois through Harriet Converse Maxwell, an activist on behalf of Indian rights. This trip, which may have been Heye's first formal visit to an Indian community (fig. 43), initiated a tradition of buying trips that lasted for fifty years.[7] During the next few years Heye acquired objects from individual Natives and began to purchase collections. Later he obtained many photographs as part of the artifact collections he bought.

Heye continued his program of self-education in 1904 by consulting George Hubbard Pepper,

45. Eastern Cherokee woman gathering corn, 1908. North Carolina. Photo by Mark R. Harrington. N2736

then an assistant curator at the American Museum of Natural History and a founder of the American Anthropological Association. In describing this first meeting to the eminent anthropologist Frederick Webb Hodge, Pepper wrote, "I think he is to be one of our most earnest workers [in anthropology]."[8] Pepper also noted that Heye had just joined the American Anthropological Association as a member, had ordered all the back issues of its journal, and appeared to be ready to contribute funds to publish research.

Through Pepper, Heye soon met Marshall H. Saville, a professor of archaeology at Columbia University. Recognizing Heye's financial resources and enthusiasm, Saville encouraged Heye's interests in an effort to secure support and funding for archaeological and scientific research (fig. 44).[9] Heye later credited Pepper and Saville with teaching him the fundamentals of scientific method and technique. According to Heye's biographer and longtime associate J. Alden Mason, "It was primarily from these two men that he learned the importance of systematic collecting, scientific recording, and the proper preservation of specimens."[10]

Although Mason does not specifically mention photography, the scientific recording Heye learned about most likely included the use of the camera as an essential aid for research purposes. By the turn of the twentieth century, the camera had already been in use on scientific exploring expeditions for almost fifty years. The introduction of flexible roll-films and portable cameras in the late 1880s made it even simpler for scientists, including anthropologists, to take cameras into the field. By World War I the camera was a standard part of field equipment.[11]

Anthropologists and archaeologists relied on the camera to provide an objective and accurate document of perceived reality. While ethnographers depended on the camera primarily for its illustrative abilities, archaeologists actually integrated the camera into their methodology, using it as a tool to count, compare, and measure archaeological features.[12] When Heye met him, Pepper was already an experienced photographer who had created hundreds of photographs for his archaeological and ethnological research in the Southwest.

Almost immediately after their meeting, Pepper carried out a modest expedition to Michoacán for Heye. In 1906 Saville directed site excavations in Ecuador on an expedition underwritten by Heye's mother Marie Antoinette Heye. Pepper supervised the excavations and made documentary photographs that are most likely *among* the first, if not *the* first, images in Heye's collection. These excavations provided new information about the extent of pre-

Columbian cultures in Ecuador. Objects collected on that expedition form one of the largest holdings of early Ecuadoran artifacts outside Central America.[13]

In 1907 the American Anthropological Association determined that Latin America was a region in critical need of research, thus reflecting the United States' emerging interest in hemispheric affairs in the wake of the Spanish-American War in 1898.[14] With Saville's advice, Heye sponsored research in Latin America, sending Pepper to Mexico, Frank Utley to Puerto Rico, and Saville to Ecuador.[15] Over the next twenty years Heye financed substantial archaeological and ethnological research in Latin America, which resulted in sizable groups of artifacts and photographs entering the collection.

46. Oneida family portrait, 1907. Ontario, Canada. Photo by Mark R. Harrington. N2641

47. Seminole men, ca. 1910. Photo by Alanson B. Skinner. N1504

As his interest in collecting grew, Heye hired recent Columbia graduate Mark Raymond Harrington to work for him in 1908. Initially Harrington, who later became curator of the Southwest Museum in Los Angeles, carried out field work along the eastern seaboard, in the South and Midwest, and in Cuba. Among the tribes he visited were the Mohegan, Pamunkey and Mattaponi, the Cherokee in North Carolina (fig. 45), and the Catawba and Seminole, as well as the Choctaw, Chitimacha, Houma, Koasati, and Alibamu in Texas. In Oklahoma he researched the Lenape (Delaware), Shawnee, Sac and Fox, Kickapoo, Kiowa, Comanche, Apache, Wyandot, Caddo, and Wichita, among others.[16] Harrington, who was credited with collecting more artifacts for Heye than any other anthropologist, later conducted extensive archaeological field work in Arkansas and in Nevada.[17] Following the visual conventions of the era, his photographs rely on a mid-range perspective that is neither too intimate nor too distant but instead records a great amount of ethnographic detail (fig. 46). Harrington, like his colleagues, was particularly interested in recording the context in which he had collected artifacts and data, often showing people wearing or using the actual objects.

As the result of these many expeditions, Heye's collection of Indian artifacts grew tremendously. He initially kept his collection in his home, but eventually he was forced to seek larger accommodations. After the collection outgrew a succession of commercial spaces in New York, Heye made arrangements with the University of Pennsylvania for the University Museum to house a large portion of his objects. In turn, Heye became a member of the museum's board of directors, and with the weight of his patronage behind him, he began to define the University Museum's research agenda. Under Heye's sponsorship, several young anthropologists, including Harrington, Frank G. Speck, and Alanson Buck Skinner, were hired to conduct ethnological and archaeological research. Pepper also joined the staff and supervised the installation of an exhibition of Heye's collection at the University Museum. These anthropologists, many of whom would forge distinguished careers, energetically pursued research and collecting for Heye (fig. 47).

During these years Heye was keenly interested in establishing his own credentials as a "gentleman" archaeologist, and he began to participate in excavations. In 1914 Heye and his crew were arrested for robbing graves while excavating a Munsee–Lenape (Delaware) burial ground in New Jersey. Convicted and fined, Heye successfully appealed his sentence to the New Jersey Supreme Court, later stating that he did so to protect archaeologists' rights to conduct excavations for scientific purposes without fear of legal sanctions.[18] The next year Heye took his new bride, Thea Kowne Page, to Nacoochee Mound in Georgia, where she spent her honeymoon in dungarees while he excavated burial sites.

THE MUSEUM'S HEYDAY

When Heye's mother died in 1915, Heye inherited the bulk of his father's estate of nearly $10,000,000. He had earlier given up his banking and industrial interests to devote himself more fully to collecting, and he now zealously embarked on building an institution. Heye decided to create and endow his own museum, establishing himself as chairman of the board of trustees and director for life, and retaining control of the museum with the right to appoint all board members. Early members were men much like Heye, wealthy individuals with an avid interest in Indians but with no time for academic study.[19] Two of the most influential trustees were Harmon W. Hendricks, owner of a metalwork firm, and James B. Ford, vice president of the United States Rubber Company. Together they financed a large portion of the museum's annual payroll and presented generous donations of singular artifacts and entire collections.

Heye built a museum to house his collection with the assistance of philanthropist Archer M. Huntington, who donated land and funds for construction. The Beaux-Arts complex already included the Hispanic Society of America and the American Geographical Society. Built on land in northern Manhattan formerly owned by the family of naturalist John James Audubon, the new museum at Audubon Terrace was ready for occupancy in 1917. The building, however, was requisitioned for military purposes during World War I, and it did not open to the public until 1922.

48. Tzutujil Maya, 1928. Lake Atitlán, Guatemala. Photo by Samuel K. Lothrop. N14113

Around this time Heye hired Edwin F. Coffin, a former race car driver who became the museum's first official photographer. The two met when the Pierce-Arrow automobile company sent Coffin along as a chauffeur for the car that Heye had purchased for one of his nearly annual cross-country collecting trips. Heye took a liking to Coffin and "gave him a field commission as an anthropologist." Coffin became a capable archaeological photographer and later carried out archaeological field work in Texas for Heye.[20] He served as photographer until 1932, when Heye released most of his staff after he encountered financial problems.[21]

The first major expedition undertaken after the museum's creation was the Hendricks-Hodge Expedition (1916–23) to excavate the ancestral Zuni pueblos of Hawikku and Kechiba:wa. Along with thousands of artifacts and many burials, the expedition generated more than a thousand archaeological and ethnological photographs in one of the most systematic anthropological projects ever mounted. Directed by Frederick Webb Hodge, the expedition visited the sites as well as Zuni Pueblo and its outlying farming village of Ojo Caliente during six field seasons.

While the expedition photographers were extraordinarily successful in documenting the excavations and everyday life in Zuni, they sometimes faced strong objections to their attempts to photograph community members. Writing to Hodge in 1919, Jesse Nusbaum complained, "Spent the day in Zuni getting pictures . . . and think that I have a pretty good series altho [sic] not all that I wanted to get by any means. Many didn't care to have pictures taken at all—even at Ojo—many wouldn't stand for it. But with what I have from previous visits Zuni and these— think you can get what you want [for the publication *Zuni Breadstuff*]. . . ."[22]

By 1917 a sizable collection of photographs had been amassed at the Museum of the American Indian (MAI). While Heye personally catalogued every artifact until he retired as director in 1955, he left the care and cataloguing of the photographs to his assistants and secretaries.[23] Pepper created the first catalogue of the collection, which by then numbered more than 1,500 negatives.[24]

Over the next few years Heye recruited some of the best anthropological talent of the era, hiring Frederick Hodge away from the Bureau of Ethnology and Marshall Saville away from Columbia University in 1918, and employing Samuel K. Lothrop, a Harvard graduate, in 1923. Lothrop, who later became curator at Harvard's Peabody Museum of Archaeology and Ethnology, was both a brilliant archaeologist and a talented photographer. He carried out research on textiles and pottery in Guatemala and El Salvador (fig. 48), and led excavations in Tierra del Fuego, where he photographed the indigenous community that did not survive the twentieth century as a distinct culture.

Another early staff member was Donald A. Cadzow, who participated in the Hendricks-Hodge Expedition and conducted ethnological work in northern Canada. Cadzow, whose uncle Daniel Cadzow established the Rampart House trading post only eighty miles from the Arctic Circle, apparently was hired after he brought a collection of Inuit and Athapaskan materials to New York around 1916. Over the next ten years Cadzow returned to Canada on several collecting and research trips for Heye.[25] Little is known about his training or experience, but Cadzow may

49. Pokiak (Eskimo [Inuit]), ca. 1917. Mackenzie Delta, Northwest Territories, Canada. Photo by Donald A. Cadzow. N2023

have learned photography from his uncle. Cadzow's works reflect his eclectic interest in his surroundings and often express a warm relationship between photographer and subject (fig. 49).

Heye also hired independent individuals from a variety of backgrounds, such as artist A. Hyatt Verrill, who was familiar with Latin America, salesman and clerk Willem Wildschut, who specialized in Absaroke (Crow) and Mandan objects, and hotel proprietor Edward H. Davis, who traveled throughout California, Arizona, and northern Mexico. These men were typically mavericks who developed close relationships with certain Indian communities, and they all demonstrated a particular facility with the camera.

Verrill was among Heye's most colorful collectors, a man who styled himself as an adventurer and explorer in the flamboyant tradition of popular literature and film. Trained as an artist, he attended the Yale School of Fine Arts, and at age seventeen he went to Dominica to collect fauna specimens for the Yale Museum. There he encountered Caribs while he was obtaining examples of local animals. He took up photography in the 1890s and established a professional studio and photography business with a specialty in photographing natural history.

The two men met around 1905, and Verrill began to collect for Heye in the Caribbean and South America. Over the next twenty years he made ethnological and archaeological trips in British Guiana, Panama, Bolivia, Peru, and Chile (fig. 50). Verrill's unpublished autobiography is replete with stories of blood brother ceremonies, cannibals, and lost tribes and ancient cities. Writing of his experiences with the Sirionos in Bolivia, Verrill commented that "had it not been for my pictures they would have been considered mythical."[26] In 1926 Heye abruptly dismissed Verrill when he came to the conclusion that the photographer was somehow taking advantage of him.

Another field agent who created an important photographic collection was Willem Wildschut, a Dutch immigrant in Billings, Montana, who developed a fascination with the Absaroke (Crow) living on the nearby reservation.[27] Wildschut assembled substantial collections of artifacts and ceremonial material for Heye for nearly ten years, and he prepared manuscripts that later formed the basis for publications on beadwork and medicine bundles.

Wildschut photographed the Crow extensively, taking more than 230 photographs in his role as a field collector for Heye (see figs. 6, 183). His interest in the local Indians may have been driv-

50. Patamona woman weaving beaded apron, 1917. British Guiana. Photo by A. Hyatt Verrill. N10080

en by deeply personal, perhaps spiritual, concerns. Some years after his death, Wildschut's wife Ellen recalled, "While a child Willem used to dream about Indians. . . . When the contact with the Crows was first established, it opened for him a door. . . . The years spent working with the Indians and the Museum were certainly the most rewarding of his life. When the door closed, a phaze [sic] of life died."[28] When Heye dismissed him along with many other field collectors in 1928, Wildschut was so heartbroken that he packed up his notes and cameras, and never photographed Native people again.

The early 1920s were idyllic years at the museum. Sufficient funds were available to support a wide variety of research programs and substantial collecting from all parts of the Americas. Hodge, the preeminent editor and anthropologist of his day, supervised the museum's publication program, producing both formal research reports and brief articles to inform readers of the museum's activities. According to one associate, "Until the Depression [Heye] collected the best anthropologists as well as the best artifacts, and his place was a dream come true. His crew had the money to dig up or buy up everything the rest of us couldn't afford."[29]

When the Museum of the American Indian formally opened to the public in 1922, selections from its collection of more than 100,000 artifacts were put on view. By 1924 the photographic collection contained 9,656 negatives and 6,559 prints, and included a large number of vintage nineteenth-century prints and expedition photographs. The collection by then also held more than 30,000 feet of motion picture film.[30] This substantial collection well exceeded the capabilities of the new building. Two years later Heye obtained from Archer M. Huntington additional acreage in the Bronx to build a research branch. Huntington also provided land next to his own library in the Bronx for a wing to house Heye's book and manuscript collection.

As the reputation of Heye's collection grew, private individuals began to donate their personal collections to the museum. In 1925 the children of General Nelson A. Miles donated his collection of Native American memorabilia and photographs. Miles, who was famed for his participation in successful campaigns against Tatanka Yotanka (Sitting Bull) and Goyathlay (Geronimo) at the end of the nineteenth century, had acquired many noteworthy artifacts and photographs of notable Indian leaders.

Other important donations included official photographs of Indian delegations taken by the renowned photographer Alexander Gardner and presented by P. Tecumseh Sherman, a relative of General William Tecumseh Sherman (see fig. 132). In contrast, Elizabeth C. Grinnell, wife of conservationist and Indian rights activist George Bird Grinnell, contributed photographs that reflect the intimate friendship and trust the Northern and Southern Cheyenne accorded to her and her husband in the early 1900s. The Grinnells enjoyed a longstanding relationship with these communities and were considered as son and daughter by tribal members.[31] George Bird Grinnell, who went on to publish several volumes on Cheyenne life, religion, and military history that were illustrated with his wife's photographs, regularly intervened on their behalf in disputes with government officials and neighboring white settlers, and he remained a staunch advocate for the Cheyenne until his death in 1935.

In these images Elizabeth Grinnell depicts many aspects of early reservation life for Cheyenne women in Montana and Oklahoma (fig. 51). Unlike many photographs of Plains women that tend to show them as static accessories to male warriors, Grinnell's images present the active lives of her Cheyenne friends as they gather wood and berries, ride on horseback, and care for their families. Grinnell may have emphasized this side of Indian life because she was expected to spend more time with women in accordance with Cheyenne social conventions, or she may have been particularly interested in the activities of women, whom George Bird Grinnell identified as the heart of Cheyenne camp life.[32] In a 1904 diary entry describing a trip to the Tongue River reservation, George Bird Grinnell observed, "To the great joy of the women and children Elizabeth took photos of the sweathouse on the way to the Tongue River at wood cutter camp. Little Sun was with the sweathouse and would like a photo if they are good."[33]

Heye began to purchase other large photographic collections as the 1920s progressed. In 1928 he acquired more than 3,300 negatives from Dr. Frederick Starr, an anthropologist at the University of Chicago who increased public awareness of anthropology through his lectures and books. Most of the negatives document Starr's research in Mexico on a series of field expeditions from 1897 to 1901, in the waning days of the authoritarian regime of Porfirio Diaz. His findings were published in the popular book *In Indian Mexico* (1908) and in a series of scholarly monographs (fig. 52). Starr also conducted research in Indian communities in Massachusetts and New York (fig. 53).

51. Cheyenne woman scraping hide, ca. 1902. Colony, Oklahoma. Photo by Elizabeth C. Grinnell. N13597

52. Mexican men, ca. 1900. Frederick Starr Collection. N17238

53. Staged scene of couple making cornhusk mats, ca. 1894. Onondaga, New York. Frederick Starr Collection. N15289

Starr, who pioneered the use of photography in ethnography, hired professional photographers Charles B. Lang and Louis Grabic to record these trips.[34] He was interested in documenting the "unknown" Indian in Mexico by measuring and comparing physical types, making craniometric studies of several populations, and producing detailed visual records of Indian and mestizo communities. In his travel accounts, Starr tells of Indian resistance to his project, despite his letters of authorization from federal, state, and municipal officials. In many instances male subjects had to be threatened with prison before they would agree to be measured. In San Cristobal in Chiapas, the Chamula women refused to participate for several days because they feared to be photographed. Local authorities finally confiscated their *chamaras* (a kind of outergarment) before the women would submit. "Putting the garments out of reach, the women were told by the officials, that each would receive back her property as soon as the strangers made their desired measurements." Nonetheless, a near riot ensued after attempts were made to detain the women from leaving. They finally fled screaming before Starr's assistants could make any photographs.[35] Despite his evident belief that these Indians had no right to refuse to participate in his research, Starr asserted that "the prosperity of Mexico rests more upon the indian blood than on any other element of national power."[36]

54. Eskimos (Inuits) in kayaks, 1930. Angmagsalik, East Greenland. Ford-Bartlett Expedition. N36485

THE COLLECTION DIVERSIFIES

In late March 1928 trustees James B. Ford and Harmon W. Hendricks died within days of one another. Although Heye had expected both to leave generous bequests to the museum, he was greatly disappointed in their gifts. Without their annual support, Heye was forced to choose between continuing the museum's research programs or purchasing additional collections. One month later he chose the latter. He fired most of the professional staff, thereby ending what had been "an anthropologist's dream," a life of field work, research, and publication without the burden of teaching. In this decision Heye revealed that his true motivation was acquiring artifacts. From the beginning he had noted the strengths and weaknesses of his holdings, and he repeatedly urged his field agents to acquire the specimens needed to form a comprehensive collection.[37]

The financial difficulties created by the Great Depression further strained the museum's resources in the late 1920s and early 1930s, but Heye continued to purchase collections that came on the market. By the early 1930s Heye was once again underwriting limited archaeological and ethnographic research, such as the Ford-Bartlett Expedition to excavate sites in Angmagssalik, Greenland (fig. 54).

55. Tsátchela (Colorado) mother and child, ca. 1936. Pichincha Province, Ecuador. Victor Wolfgang von Hagen Expedition. N36734

56. Mandan store interior, ca. 1910. Fort Berthold reservation, North Dakota. Photo by Fred R. Meyer. N22005

The donation and purchase of these collections slowly began to change the overall character of Heye's photographic collection. It became more varied as it grew to include commercial and tourist photography as well as images taken by artists, missionaries, and other amateur photographers. Ever the generalist, Heye apparently accepted anything, from a postcard or snapshot to a professional portrait or an official delegation view, as long as it depicted Indians.

Heye also became associated with naturalist and zoologist Dr. Victor Wolfgang von Hagen, who traveled widely in South America on expeditions to the Amazon and the Andes. In 1936 Von Hagen spent several weeks collecting floral and faunal specimens from the Tsátchela, or Colorado, Indians in the lowlands of Ecuador. (This name derived from their practice of coating their bodies and hair with orange achiote paste.) Von Hagen, who made several early films of South American Indians, was notably impressed by the sensibility of the Tsátchela, observing, "The Colorado are a people of exemplary character whose sense of honesty the white man would do well to emulate" (fig. 55).[38]

Among the collections Heye acquired in the 1930s were photographs by Frederick Johnson and Fred R. Meyer. Johnson made photographs in the 1920s and 1930s in a number of Indian communities in Canada, including the Golden Lake Algonquian in Ontario, the Mistassini in Quebec, and the Mi'kmaq in Nova Scotia (see fig. 181). His images depart from anthropological and scientific conventions in their intimacy and diverse points of view.

In 1939 Mrs. Fred R. Meyer donated 860 photographs taken by her husband of Absaroke (Crow), Blackfoot, and Mandan people in Montana and North Dakota. Little is known about Meyer, but he apparently was associated in some way, perhaps as a clerk, with the Indian agencies that served these tribes. His photographs, taken from 1903 to 1910, document many aspects of reservation life (fig. 56). Heye appreciated this donation so much that Mrs. Meyer was named a lifetime museum member.

A donation made in 1934 from the estate of Mary E. Harriman included one of the souvenir albums that documented the 1899 Harriman Alaska Expedition organized by her father E. H. Harriman, head of the Union Pacific Railroad. The expedition brought together some of the finest scientists, naturalists, and artists of the day, including C. Hart Merriam, George Bird Grinnell, John Muir, Frederick S. Dellenbaugh, and Louis Agassiz, to explore the coast of Alaska during a two-month expedition. Mary Harriman, then a teenager, accompanied the expedition along with her mother and siblings. Edward S. Curtis and his assistant D. J. Inverarity served as expedition photographers. Curtis' work on the expedition and the growth of his friendship with Grinnell ultimately led to his life project, the twenty volumes of *The North American Indians* and the twenty portfolios illustrating the lives of Native Americans in eighty tribes. A Tlingit house front that expedition members had taken from the abandoned village of Cape Fox also came with the Harriman donation.

Unlike his later elegiac portraits of Native people, the photographs of Indians that Curtis made during the expedition document the decline of Native communities and the impact of acculturation as seen in the abandoned coastal villages and ramshackle sealing camps (fig. 57; see

57. Tlingit sealers, 1899. Glacier Bay,
Alaska. Photo by Edward S. Curtis.
Harriman Alaska Expedition.
Presented by the estate of Mary E.
Harriman. N36573

fig. 137). At the same time his photographs of the Alaskan landscape have been praised for their
use of the luminous northern light, which anticipates an aesthetic later refined by Ansel Adams.[39]

Among other donations made at this time was a bequest of more than 500 photographs from
the estate of DeCost Smith, a New York artist known for his publications and drawings of
Indian subjects. Smith seems to have traveled widely in the West and visited Indian communities
near his home in Amenia, New York, in the late nineteenth and early twentieth centuries. He
took photographs and collected images for his own interest. As an artist, Smith's works reflect
an interest in composition and spontaneity that diverges markedly from the documentary concerns of anthropologists (fig. 58; see figs. 154, 187).

By the 1940s Heye's level of acquisitions began to taper off, although he continued to make
cross-country trips in search of additional objects for his collection. The daily administration of
the museum increasingly fell to Heye's assistant E. K. Burnett. By then fewer images were also
being made of Native Americans, at least in North America. Anthropologists increasingly con-

58. Bannock women beading garments, 1892. Fort Hall Reservation, Idaho. Bequest of DeCost Smith. N37128

ducted field work outside the United States, as research funding followed U.S. foreign policy interests to Africa, Asia, and Latin America.

One of Heye's few large acquisitions in the 1940s was of some 377 photographs documenting the 1941 Wenner-Gren Expedition to study the Yagua, Uitoto, Bora, and Mashco in the Peruvian Amazon (fig. 59). The photographs accompanied an array of artifacts collected from these tribes and deposited at the MAI by the Wenner-Gren Foundation. Dr. Paul Fejos, the foundation's director and the expedition's leader, was a Hungarian who was trained as an anthropologist. After he arrived in the United States, Fejos worked as a bacteriologist and then as a film director for MGM and Universal Studios. He believed that filming the Indians with sound-motion film was essential to record their cultures accurately. Working with cameraman Norman Matthews, Fejos took extensive 35mm footage during the expedition, and he often asked Indians to re-create scenes from their historical or mythic past. His description of the filmmaking process raises questions about who may have been in control of the images created.

In time, we succeeded in obtaining the active cooperation of all members of the Ant clan in taking sound-motion pictures. The shaman acted as "director" and realized by himself the necessity of rehearsing "scenes" and assigning "roles" in advance in order to avoid confusion. I myself made no attempt to influence the action or create the scenes, and only saw to it that the "actors" appeared when there was plenty of sunshine and stood within range of the camera. The Yagua, with the exception of Unchi [the shaman] who took his duties as director very seriously, found it vastly amusing to re-enact their cultural traditions and customs. Besides, as we provided for most of their needs while pictures were being taken, they enjoyed a more or less extended holiday.[40]

The photographs deposited at the NMAI are stills taken from these films.

PUBLIC ACCESS AND PRESERVATION

In 1955 Heye retired as director after he suffered a series of debilitating strokes. Acting Director E. K. Burnett hired Dr. Frederick J. Dockstader, an anthropologist on the faculty at Dartmouth College, as assistant director. After Heye's death in 1957, Dockstader became director. The museum then embarked on a five-year renovation program to refurbish all the exhibitions and to create more visible forms of public outreach.

59. Unchi (Yagua) Indian face-painting, 1941. Border of Brazil, Colombia, and Peru. Presented by the Wenner-Gren Expedition. P15553

No official photographer had been on the museum's staff since Coffin departed in 1932. The care and cataloging of the collections, as well as the making of photographs from negatives, were left to the attention of any interested staff member.[41] To reaffirm an institutional commitment to the collection, Dockstader formally re-created the photography department and named Carmelo Guadagno, then assistant to curator William Stiles, as museum photographer. Guadagno headed the department for almost twenty-five years. His skilled use of the large-format camera played an important role in making the museum's collections better known throughout the world (fig. 60). Looking back at that era, Dockstader observed, "I believe strongly that Carmelo Guadagno developed into one of the foremost museum photographers of his time, and that he has never been accorded the recognition due him."[42]

Almost immediately Dockstader sought out funds for photographic equipment and supplies, instituted a program to photograph the collections, and created color slides for sale to scholars and the public. He also began to solicit and purchase photographs for the collection. "I did go out of my way to acquire given bodies of photographic material, quite apart from material culture, for I personally valued the photo archives as one of the great strengths of the Museum."[43] One of the earliest donations

60. Maya ceramic figure, 900–1200 A.D. Guaymil Island, State of Campeche, Mexico. Height 35 cm. Photo by Carmelo Guadagno (artifact #23.2573). N31194

61. Children watching Hopi ceremony, holding dolls just given to them by Katsinas, 1919. Walpi, Arizona. Photo by Emry Kopta. Emry Kopta Collection. N27794

was a group of more than 1,500 photographs taken by Colonel Frank C. Churchill and his wife Clara from 1899 to 1909. Churchill was an outspoken proponent of assimilation and the Christianization of Indians, and he served as a special advisor to President Theodore Roosevelt. With his wife, Churchill visited nearly every reservation from the Arctic to Florida and from the East to the West Coasts during a series of appointments as inspector of the U.S. Indian agencies.

Another important collection acquired by Dockstader was formed by artist Emry Kopta in the Hopi pueblos from 1912 to 1924. Trained in San Francisco and Paris as a sculptor, Kopta lived and worked for more than twelve years at First Mesa with a Hopi family that adopted him. While living as part of the community he made more than two hundred photographs of the Hopi, ranging from scenes of everyday life to religious ceremonies (fig. 61).[44] According to his wife Anna, Kopta was held in such high esteem that he was permitted to take photographs even in the kivas.

After her husband's death, Anna Kopta decided that the collection should be divided. She gave the photographs of daily life to the Museum of Northern Arizona in Flagstaff and sent the ceremonial photographs to New York City, with the proviso that none of the ceremonial images be published during the lifetimes of any of the subjects. In recent years Hopi cultural

62. *A Canyon Patriarch* (Havasupai), ca. 1912. Grand Canyon, Arizona. Fred Harvey Collection. T6167

63. The potter Nampeyo (Hopi), after 1900 (?). Fred Harvey Collection. N31836

authorities have requested that the NMAI not allow the publication of any ceremonial photographs. Prior to that, however, scholars and Hopi community groups published the collection for research and fundraising purposes.

The MAI's collection of Southwest photography continued to grow throughout the 1960s. In 1963, the Fred Harvey Company donated a large body of glass diapositives and other photographs relating to its Southwest Indian cultural tourism program. These commercial images were among the thousands of photographs that played a key role in the early part of this century in forming the public perception of Southwest Native people, the Pueblo in particular (figs. 62, 63).[45]

In 1962 the MAI received a grant from the National Science Foundation to preserve its deteriorating collection of nitrate-based motion picture and still negative films. This preservation project led to a second funded proposal in 1965 to copy additional nitrate-based and glass-plate negatives and to create a revised catalogue of the collection. As this pioneering work went on throughout the 1960s, Guadagno continued to photograph the MAI's artifact collection, ultimately building a list of more than 2,000 color images of the collection.

It became a challenge for the museum to catalogue all its photographs, not to mention its artifacts, because the collections had largely been neglected from the 1930s to the 1950s. In 1960 Dockstader commented,

> Any big museum can't help containing a lot of things that haven't yet been accurately classified. In a way, that's its justification. There are hundreds of years of profitable research and discovery still to be put in on this [the artifact] collection. Our job isn't to pin everything down for all time, but to make it accessible to a large number of people, who will make their own discoveries.[46]

In that era it was more important that the museum staff identify the tribal group or locale accurately than record the photographer's name and the history of the image. Consequently, today we are challenged to clarify, or even to research and establish, missing or erroneous attributions in order to achieve a clear understanding of particular images or artifacts.

As a result of its efforts to preserve the collection and make it accessible to the public, the museum has become a popular source of images for scholars and publishers, especially for textbooks and other educational publications. After the American Indian Movement took over Wounded Knee, South Dakota, in 1973, the museum was flooded with requests for images. According to Guadagno, the museum supplied many of the nation's newspapers with historic photographs of the original massacre at Wounded Knee (see fig. 19).[47] This and similar incidents exemplify the continuing power of photographs of Indians to capture the public imagination, and the museum's role as an institutional broker of such images to shape public understanding.

Under Dockstader the museum also revived its research program on a limited scale. Museum staff initiated ethnological projects among the Naskapi and Montagnais, and archaeological excavations in Tennessee. Outside research associates took on special projects in the Southwest. Among the most comprehensive undertakings was Ernest and Eloise Carter's program to document sites of Native American petroglyphs and pictographs in California, Nevada, and the Southwest. For more than five years the Carters traveled to remote sites to document this prehistoric art, and they annually shipped scores of negatives and color slides to the museum. In the 1970s Guadagno accompanied professional potter Lewis Krevolin on a month-long research trip to Mexico to document indigenous pottery techniques. The project created an archive of more than 500 images (fig. 64).

Like any institution, the museum prefers to obtain well-documented photographs, but on occasion it has acquired important but poorly documented collections. Among the most intriguing are the David C. Vernon collection (see figs. 71, 130), donated by Laurance Rockefeller in 1972, and the Charles Rau collection (fig. 65). These collections contain a variety of visually

64. Mexican potter firing pottery, ca. 1973. Amatenango, Chiapas, Mexico. Photo by Carmelo Guadagno.

65. Thompson or Lilooet man dipnet fishing from platform; fish drying racks are in the background. Fraser River, British Columbia, Canada. Charles Rau Collection. N36415

provocative images of different tribal groups, and they include examples of early photographic processes from the nineteenth century. In most cases little information on the photographer or date of the image is available.

CHANGING PERSPECTIVES

In the 1970s changing social attitudes of and toward Native Americans began to influence the kinds of images created and thus made available to the museum. While non-Indians continued to photograph Native Americans, they could no longer take for granted their right to make images, and thus represent Native individuals or their culture. For their part, Native Americans no longer felt obligated to permit their photographs to be taken, and many reservation communities restricted photography in different ways. (Some reservations had begun to restrict photography as early as the 1920s.) A concurrent resurgence of romantic nostalgia for "lost" Indian culture both popularized a certain kind of historic image and led to the emergence of decorative commercial photography. As a result, the character of contemporary photography of Indians distinctly differs from that encountered as little as forty years before.

After nearly twenty years Dockstader left the museum in 1977, and Dr. Roland Force, an anthropologist and former director of the Bishop Museum in Honolulu, became director the following year. A new generation of museum staff initiated public programs that increasingly focused on the needs and interests of Native Americans. In 1979 Elizabeth Weatherford and Emelia Seubert organized the first Native American Film and Video Festival featuring not only media about but also by Native Americans. Later the Film and Video Department was formally established, thereby separating the administration of the collections of still and moving images. This presentation of Native perspectives in media anticipated a growing trend in the museum's programming in the 1980s, as Native Americans became more involved as interpreters of their material and cultural heritage.

The preservation of the photography collection reemerged as a primary concern under my direction as assistant curator of photography. The museum received several grants from federal and private agencies to rehouse photographs in appropriate archival materials and to install climate control systems to maintain proper environmental conditions. Funds were also secured to develop computerized cataloging systems to improve public and institutional access to the photographs.

Although the museum essentially ceased to collect photography after the 1970s, it did continue to accept donations. In 1984 Shirley Glubok Tamarin, a noted author of children's books, donated a collection of black-and-white photographs made by her late husband Alfred Tamarin. These images, made during a series of visits to Indian communities along the East Coast in the early 1970s, were the basis for the book *We Have Not Vanished: Eastern Indians of the United States* (1974). Tamarin dedicated these images to the premise that Indian communities not only have survived, but they also continue to be a vital presence in the modern world.

In a surprising echo of the past, the museum received in 1984 a donation of 183 of the 2,200 copper photogravure plates used to create Edward S. Curtis' monumental *North American Indians* (see fig. 141). Some years earlier the plates had been discovered in an antique store after decades of obscurity. Although Curtis had intended to create 500 bound sets of his life's work, only 272 were actually made in his lifetime. After efforts to complete the publication of the bound volumes or to market new prints commercially proved unsuccessful, investors decided to break up the collection of plates and donate them to various repositories, including the Museum of the American Indian.

During these years the museum also hosted several exhibitions of contemporary photography, such as Toba Tucker's photographs of the Navajo (fig. 66) and Susanne Page's photographs of the Hopi. In 1986 I campaigned to bring *Silver Drum*, an exhibition of photography by Native Americans, to the museum. Organized by the Native Indian/Inuit Photographers' Association in Ontario, Canada, the exhibition featured the work of five Native American photographers, including Richard W. Hill, Sr. This exhibition, held some seventy years after Heye began his collection, marked the first inclusion of the Native perspective into the museum's presentation of still photography. The works on view, which represented a totality of Native American humanity rather than a mere documentation of Native American culture, asserted a new set of values and standards to be used in viewing images of Native peoples. Since becoming a part of the Smithsonian Institution in 1992, the museum has developed plans to build its holdings of photography by Native Americans in order to fulfill its new expanded mission to present and interpret the perspectives of Native peoples themselves.

IMAGING THE FUTURE

At a time when public interest in the American Indian was waning and Native Americans were thought to be on the verge of cultural, if not physical, extermination, George Gustav Heye embarked on a mission to create the world's largest collection of objects made by and representing Native Americans. In doing so, he greatly contributed to the preservation of the Native heritage for future generations. It is an irony of history that Heye is said to have held little interest in the well-being of living Native people. One associate recalled, "He didn't give a hang about Indians and he never seemed to have heard about their problems in present-day society."[48] Nonetheless, the photography collection he initiated permits a wide range of discussions concerning the nature of Native culture and how it should be represented and presented.

With few exceptions, most of the anecdotal information available about particular views or photographers comes from the makers, rather than the subjects, of the images. The NMAI's photography department recently has begun to host visits by tribal delegations interested in seeing photographs that pertain to their communites. Perhaps in a few years it will be possible to present a more comprehensive discussion of these photographs from both sides of the camera lens.

66. Bernice Begay (Navajo) and Bah Chee (Navajo), mother and daughter, 16 May 1981. Jeddito Island, Arizona. Photo by Toba P. Tucker. P23390

Contemplating these images of Native peoples challenges the viewer to consider sources of authenticity and the meaning of stereotypes. In writing about the work of Edward S. Curtis, whose photographs have been the subject of much contemporary criticism for their romantic sensibilities, NMAI curator George Horse Capture observed that such historic images (including one that Curtis made of his great-grandfather) can hold great meaning for Indian people. "Real Indians are extremely grateful to see what their ancestors look like or what they did and we know they are not stereotypes. No one staged the people. And we see them at their classic finest."[49] Clearly, the interpretations and issues associated with these photographs must be negotiated image by image, and these works provide a rich ground to investigate and contest them.

Heye's Strategy

*Photographs Record
Material Acquisitions*

Pamela Dewey

George Gustav Heye dedicated his life and inherited wealth to acquiring the material culture of Native Americans of North and South America. One of the primary vehicles for acquisition was his funded expeditions of ethnographers and anthropologists. These expeditions generated an enormous amount of photographic material, with visual records of excavation sites, the landscape and people encountered, and the artifacts that he purchased. Most of the unique images in the archive resulted from the Heye-sponsored expeditions that took place during the early part of this century, prior to 1930. In terms of strict historical and chronological representation, the archive collection is inconsistent, but to see it as simply an incomplete historical record overlooks Heye's original intention for the photographs. They were taken to support the *artifacts* being acquired and to increase their value as authentic examples of Native American material culture.

As Heye amassed his collection, he wanted to ensure that his acquisitions, now removed from their original function and meaning, would retain their significance in Western culture. In image

67. (opposite) Osage and Quapaw
men, before 1917. Oklahoma. The
arrow points to a man wearing
leggings (6.1013) and moccasins
(6.1014) that are now in the NMAI
collection. N37877 (P1654)

68. Shuar women wearing clothing
(18.8750, 18.8751, 18.8754, 18.8770)
that is now in the NMAI collection,
1935. Rio Bom Boisa, Upper
Amazonia, Ecuador. Photo by
Victor Wolfgang von Hagen. N36661
(P11503)

after image unnamed persons wear articles of clothing and use objects and utensils similar to those Heye had in his possession. In many instances photographs document the very item he was purchasing. One image shows a group of unnamed Osage and Quapaw men standing in a semicircle (fig. 67). One man looks down at his feet; an arrow drawn onto the photograph's surface points to him. The catalogue card indicates that his leggings and moccasins, the very ones he is wearing, are in the museum's collection as artifacts 6.1013 and 6.1014. Other photographs are similar. The caption information that accompanies a portrait of two Shuar women (fig. 68) describes only the articles of clothing and jewelry they wear. Clearly, in these cases the unnamed Native Americans are present to lend authenticity to the objects being shown.

Such expedition images form the backbone of the archive and account for thousands of images that are rarely seen or used. The archive is unique precisely because Heye did not discriminate among objects that he deemed suitable for his collection. He simply gathered *everything* in his path. Today, the NMAI Photo Archive remains an invaluable resource for images of objects being used in daily life, during a critical period of transition for Native American cultures.

A portrait of a Lenape (Delaware) man and his son at the turn of the century juxtaposes two periods of time and illustrates an era of extreme transition (fig. 69). The father is dressed in clothing of his generation. His tailored calico shirt and handmade hide trousers reflect a continuum, combining methods learned from parents and acquired from centuries of trade. New styles and materials, such as imported German glass beads, were gradually incorporated into everyday usage. The child, in stark contrast, wears a stained and ill-fitting European-style jacket and knickers transplanted from another culture.

Through centuries of trade, elements outside indigenous cultures gradually entered common usage. The photographs show the effects of trade, immigration, and modernization. It was a time when modern or foreign items were brought together with traditional products and older methods that were still in use, and influence can be seen in both directions. By 1890 many Native Americans used the same horsedrawn wagons that had brought European explorers and later photographers to the West (fig. 70). At the turn of the nineteenth century the mechanical sewing machine greatly affected the Seminole style of clothing, involving sewing together thin bands of scrap fabric (see fig. 178).[1]

Photographs document the spread of certain items across the country. Similar metal buckets and cooking pots, for example, were used by an Inuit woman in Nome, Alaska, and by a Sioux woman in the Plains (fig. 71). Even today, some of the first outside objects to enter communities in the interior regions of the Amazon are metal pots and knives, or weapons and medicine. Often items exchanged through a network of trade routes are not necessities; they may substitute for things that were already available, such as beads, which are used in the same patterns as quills. The lines of communication and trade that are maintained through exchange often are as significant as the objects themselves.[2]

Institutional forms of education and religion accompanied the Indians' dislocation from their homelands and the beginnings of reservation life. In one photograph a group of Anglo-Americans pose with two Lakota women in front of tipis and

69. Lenape (Delaware) man and son,

1906. Photo by Mark R. Harrington.

N3161

70. Navajo man, 1898. Chaco
Canyon, New Mexico. Photo by
George H. Pepper. N33064

71. Sioux (?) woman cooking. David
C. Vernon Collection. Presented by
Laurance S. Rockefeller. N41458
(P22041)

72. Sioux group in front of tipis, wagons, and boy's boarding school, 1890. Fort Bennett, South Dakota. Joseph Hurst Collection. N41461

73. Mrs. Frank C. Churchill visiting San Carlos Apache woman, 1905. Photo by Col. Frank C. Churchill. Col. Frank C. Churchill Collection. N26388

wagons (fig. 72). Standing alone in the background, as if artificially inserted into the landscape, is a large, two-story boarding school. Just as this building has been transplanted onto the landscape, the ideas it represents were meant to be incorporated into Native American cultures. One important mission of the Indian education programs run by missionaries and the Bureau of Indian Affairs was to "civilize" the Natives and to make them live as white people.[3] The pressure to conform, to "Americanize," is evident in many images of schoolchildren in boarding schools learning to adjust to European-style dress and hairstyles (see figs. 179, 180). Other images capture traditional teaching methods of sharing work with children, such as when a Montagnais man and boys divide a catch of fish.

A photograph of Clara Churchill, wife of Indian inspector Frank Churchill, visiting a San Carlos Apache woman in front of her home emphasizes the differences between the two women (fig. 73). From their contrasting styles of dress to Mrs. Churchill's refusal to sit on the ground, this staging implies that Mrs. Churchill is the observer and the Apache woman is the "other." By not sitting, however, Mrs. Churchill remains the outsider who does not attempt to relate to the woman on her own terms. In addition, the Apache woman's hands move to cover her face. Many pictures in the collection are simply labeled "woman covering her face who did not want her picture taken." The photographer, as the outsider, is actually the intruder.

The interaction and contrast between cultures appears in many different forms. Some images

74. (opposite) Ute men and women

with cowboys. N38077

75. Old George's family (Navajo),

1899. Photo by Sumner W.

Matteson, Jr. N3758

76. Quiche Maya man weaving.
Quirigua, Guatemala. United Fruit
Company. N37947

77. Quiche Maya women weaving.
Quirigua, Guatemala. United Fruit
Company. N37948

illustrate the results of integration and trade. One photo of Ute men and women with cowboys shows them wearing blankets in similar ways, which indicates that they shared a certain level of communication and interaction (fig. 74). In other instances cultural differences stand out in sharp contrast, as in a picture of Old George's family on the Navajo reservation, Chaco Canyon, New Mexico (fig. 75). Here, a family sitting on the ground eats from bowls and metal tins, while in the background, on the other side of a barbed-wire fence, a white woman holds a baby on her lap. This shows the simultaneous proximity and separation between the two cultures.

By the turn of the nineteenth century, the period most strongly represented in the collection, various aspects of the four hundred years of contact between Indian and Euroamerican cultures can be seen, particularly the influences and impositions of one culture over another. In two photographs that are catalogued as "Gift of the United Fruit Company," a Guatemalan man weaves at a bedloom (fig. 76) and Quiche Maya women work at home on traditional backstrap looms with their children nearby (fig. 77). Traditionally, and especially today, weaving is the domain of Maya women.[4] Like the pottery wheel, the bedloom was introduced by the Spanish into areas where such work formerly had been done by hand. These new mechanical tools brought about a gender difference in labor, with men using the new machinery and women continuing with traditional methods.[5] Older ways of weaving preserve and pass down from generation to generation a whole range of meaning in the designs and symbols that can be traced to the ancient Maya hieroglyphs of the Popol Vuh.[6] The woven cloth also identifies the wearer by family and village, and as being Indian.[7]

Many images in the NMAI Photo Archive are rarely used. Often those that are not selected for reproduction do not tell a particular or familiar story. They simply show people involved in

78. Kuna woman transporting bundles by canoe, 1938. Rio Diablo, Panama. Presented by Miss C. S. Edholm. N25435

79. Carrier men cleaning fish, ca.
1920. Babine, British Columbia,
Canada. Photo possibly by Lt.
G. T. Emmons. N36131

79. Carrier men cleaning fish, ca. 1920. Babine, British Columbia, Canada. Photo possibly by Lt. G. T. Emmons. N36131

their daily lives, such as a Salish woman of Fraser River tending smoked salmon or a Kuna woman transporting bundles by canoe (fig. 78). A photo of a Blackfeet camp of tipis with meat drying illustrates traditional food sources, and a view of Babine Village, British Columbia, shows an abundant catch of fish (fig. 79). In yet another photo an Eskimo woman grimaces with cold in front of a house made of bones and fur skins.

Unlike many studio photographers who produced postcard images of "typical" expressionless Indians in "exotic" clothing, others portrayed Natives as real people involved in understandable daily life activities. Stereotypical notions are perpetuated and reinforced by repetitively choosing familiar pictures, such as the famous studio portrait of Goyathlay (Geronimo) posed with a rifle (see fig. 88). The archive also contains a lesser known image in which Goyathlay, savvy to the power of the photographic image, poses with his family in a melon patch (fig. 80). Indeed, many images in the collection are similar family portraits.

80. Goyathlay (Geronimo),
Chiricahua Apache, and his family,
ca. 1895. Fort Sill, Oklahoma.
Presented by Mrs. Allyn Capron.
N37517

Photographs in the NMAI archive form a portrait of a period of intense transition and rapid modernization colliding with centuries-old ways of life. As history is reexamined, these photographs can be used to interpret the past from new directions, and overlooked images can illustrate aspects of a story that previously were not discussed. Opening up these lesser-known images to contemporary viewpoints and Native perspectives can imbue them with greater meaning and relevance to our lives today.

Photographs by
Larry McNeil

81. Charles Burton, Qinugan
Nayusian, and Barbara Elizabeth,
children of Nora and Delbert
Rexford of Barrow, Alaska, 1984.
This image illustrates the traditional
dress of the Inupiat people of the far
northern reaches of Alaska. P26511

82. A resident of the small village of
Angoon in southeast Alaska
prepares sockeye salmon in the
traditional manner, filleting the fish
and then smoking it to preserve it
for use in winter. Many Alaska
Natives continue to hunt and fish
for subsistence. P26515

83. Mrs. Kanrilak, (Yup'ik, left), and a friend (Yup'ik) gather saltwater grass at Tununak, Alaska, to make their famous coiled baskets. The grass is picked, blade by blade, just days before the snow covers the island for the season. The women are wearing fur-lined parkas with cloth shells. P26512

84. Cases of salmon are wheeled in
on rails and steamed in this massive
salmon cooker. Many Native
Alaskans make a living in the fishing
industry, as individuals or together
in tribal businesses. P26513

85. The late Maria Miller of Haines, Alaska, was one of the master Chilkat robe-makers. She is holding a dance apron; the Killer Whale Clan robe in the background is one she had recently finished. Each robe takes more than a year for a master to complete, from gathering the raw materials to dyeing, spinning, and weaving the mountain goat wool. P26514

86. A Tlingit commercial fisherman
checking his Dungeness crab trap in
Cordova, Alaska, at the formerly
Tlingit-owned Ocean Beauty
Seafoods. P26516

2. Camera Shots

Photographers,
Expeditions, and
Collections

Natasha Bonilla Martinez

with Rose Wyaco

Many factors contribute to the creation of a photographic image: the social concerns and aesthetic perspective of the photographer, the capabilities and limitations of the camera and film, the attitudes or circumstances of the subject (or surroundings of the object). When photographs depict human beings, the relationship between photographer and subject further influences the photograph's final appearance. After an image is made, its interpretation is ultimately affected by the viewer's particular interests and knowledge.

With photographs of Native Americans, the first two elements can at times be most easily understood. Photographers leave diaries and autobiographies; scholars carry out extensive research. Museum curators preserve antique cameras and can provide information on shutter speeds, exposure times, and emulsion sensitivities.

The third and fourth elements, and in particular the concerns of subjects, are more elusive. Photographers rarely were interested in what Indian people thought about being photographed. Language barriers often impeded communication, and cultural differences led to indifference and arrogant patronage. The final element—the viewer's outlook—is a matter of personal assessment.

Great photographs may need no context to be appreciated in formal terms, but most photographs of people benefit when we know something about the photographers and subjects. With such knowledge images become more than objects made of paper and chemicals. They become windows (albeit hazy ones) into history and human experience.

Today the photographic archive of the National Museum of the American Indian houses approximately 90,000 images. Some of its most significant and well-documented collections—those formed by the collector General Nelson A. Miles and the photographers Frank C. and Clara Churchill, Edward H. Davis, and Frank G. Speck, as well as the many images taken by

Detail, fig. 113.

photographers on the Hendricks-Hodge Expedition—dramatically illustrate different attitudes that have been directed towards Indians during this century. By virtue of scope and size, each of these bodies of photographs contains and conveys stories about a particular time, events, and individuals in Indian communities. Most of these images were taken between 1870 and the late 1930s, at a time when the very survival of Native Americans themselves was in question, and when many believed that Indian people would eventually be assimilated into mainstream society for the good of all concerned.

GENERAL NELSON A. MILES COLLECTION

While the NMAI's photographic collection features primarily twentieth-century works, it also contains some notable collections of nineteenth-century images. In 1925 George Heye enthusiastically accepted the donation of artifacts and more than 200 photographs collected by the famed Indian fighter General Nelson A. Miles, who built his career and reputation during the 1870s and 1880s. Three of the greatest Indian leaders—Tatanka Yotanka (Sitting Bull), Heinmot Toolalakeet (Chief Joseph), and Goyathlay (Geronimo)—had surrendered to the general.

Miles collected images of many famous Indian leaders (fig. 87), as well as other portraits and scenes, most likely from 1869 to 1892, when he was posted in the West. While his intentions are not known, the photographs serve as a trophy, a visible record of his engagements and relationships with Indian tribes and individuals. His collection brings together images by well-known frontier photographers, including A. F. Randall, John Grabill, C. S. Fly, and Stanley Morrow. These widely reproduced images present Indians and western life during and around the tumultuous years of the Indian Wars. They include portraits of leaders such as Red Cloud (see fig. 151) and Goyathlay (fig. 88), scenes of boarding school children and prisoners (see figs. 179, 180), and images of buffalo taken with one of the earliest portable cameras (see fig. 185). Many of the photographs were created for commercial purposes and were intended to inform and titillate the public fascination with all things Indian, an appetite then at its peak during the settlement of the West after the Civil War. Like Miles, these frontier photographers undoubtedly viewed Indians as an exotic and even frightening, but ultimately doomed segment of the western landscape that would eventually give way to the "wave of civilization . . . moving over the western horizon. . . . No human hand could stay that rolling tide of progress."[1]

Miles came from a long line of colonial Indian fighters in Massachusetts. After he served with distinction in the Civil War, Miles married Mary Sherman, niece of General William Tecumseh Sherman. He assumed command of the Fifth Cavalry troops stationed in Kansas, where he developed one of the "premier Indian fighting units" in the 1874–75 Red River Wars to force disaffected Kiowas, Comanches, and Cheyennes back onto their reservations.[2] Miles went on to serve in the Sioux Wars of 1876–77, where he coordinated the surrenders of several leaders, including Crazy Horse and Sitting Bull. Of the latter he recalled in his memoir, *Serving the*

87. Crow Dog (Lakota, Brulé band) and his family, 16 January 1891. Near Pine Ridge, South Dakota. Photo by John C. H. Grabill. Gen. Nelson A. Miles Collection. Presented by Maj. Sherman Miles and Mrs. Samuel Reber. P7008

88. Portrait of Goyathlay (Geronimo), Chiricahua Apache, 1887. This may be one of the earliest images of Goyathlay. Photo by A. Frank Randall or G. Ben Wittick. Gen. Nelson A. Miles Collection. Presented by Maj. Sherman Miles and Mrs. Samuel Reber. N31464 (P6842)

Republic, "Sitting Bull . . . was the embodiment of everything hostile to civilization, a perfect type of the savage Indian, a natural born leader of men, cunning and courageous. He always advocated war upon the white race. . . . He had the powers of drawing, molding, and wielding large bodies of his race and inspiring their emotions until they were prepared to act and move as one."[3]

Following the Sioux Wars, Miles joined the hunt for the disaffected Nez Percé led by Chief Joseph (see fig. 16) who were attempting to flee to Canada after their violent confrontations with white settlers and government troops. After weeks of pursuit and bitter fighting, Miles finally compelled them to surrender, promising that they eventually would be allowed to return to their homeland in the Wallowa Valley in Oregon. As would occur on other occasions, the federal government later rescinded Miles' agreement and forced the Nez Percé to Indian Territory, where many died of malarial fevers. According to Miles, "Chief Joseph was the highest type of Indian I have ever known, very handsome, kind, and brave. He was quite an orator and the idol of his tribe."[4]

Miles subsequently commanded the Department of New Mexico and Arizona after General Crook was unable to secure Goyathlay's surrender. While he found Goyathlay intimidating— "There has seldom appeared a more ruthless marauder than Geronimo. He had the most determined face and sharp, piercing eye that I had ever seen . . . "[5]—Miles convinced him to surrender after organizing a relentless pursuit in the Southwest and Mexico. Goyathlay and his followers were later deported and imprisoned in Florida for several years (see fig. 170).

During Miles' final command in the West he struggled to suppress the Ghost Dance cult, a pan-Indian religious movement that prophesied the restoration of the time before the white man's appearance, a time when the buffalo and all the Indians who had died would return. Miles attempted to prevent groups of Sioux, such as Big Foot's band, and others from gathering in the winter of 1890. He feared that such assemblies, especially if confirmed traditionalists such as Sitting Bull were present, would lead to renewed hostilities against white citizens. Miles' efforts to arrest and isolate Sitting Bull culminated in Sitting Bull's murder by tribal policemen. A short time later Miles' troops confronted Big Foot's band near Wounded Knee, and despite the surrender of most of the warriors, slaughtered more than one hundred men, women, and children as they fled through the December snow. Although several of the soldiers were later awarded the Congressional Medal of Honor, Miles always refused to defend the massacre. "I have never felt that the action was judicious or justifiable, and have always believed that it could have been avoided. It was a fatality, however, that Indian hostilities, uprisings, and wars, should finally close in a deplorable tragedy."[6]

The irony of Miles' life, and of his collection, is that he was so intimately engaged in destroying a people he at times apparently admired. Although he adopted General Sherman's brutal and often deadly methods of total warfare against Indians, Miles was at heart an assimilationist who believed the Natives could be redeemed by civilization. He advocated education and instruction in agriculture and husbandry, and endorsed policies to rescind the "protected" status of Indians on the reservation. "The sooner the Indians are, as individuals, placed on the same footing as

89. San Carlos Apache workers digging irrigation ditch, ca. 1884. San Carlos, Arizona. Photo by A. Frank Randall. Gen. Nelson A. Miles Collection. Presented by Maj. Sherman Miles and Mrs. Samuel Reber. N36006 [P6761]

others as respects their responsibility and rights and admitted to such privileges as their character and capacity may entitle them to, the sooner, in my judgment, will they cease to be a bill of expense, a source of corruption, and a disturbing element of the country."[7] In these views he prefigured a generation of reformers who would try to accomplish those very goals for nearly fifty years, from the 1880s to the 1930s.

Photographs in the Miles collection depict a period of convulsive violence between Indians and whites, in which little by little Native people lost the struggle for political power and control of their lands. Portraits of great men give way to photographs of warriors on prison trains and horsemen reduced to digging ditches (fig. 89). In many of these images, the Native American is still the unfathomable or fearsome other, the alien who in some abstract sense justifies his own dispossession.

THE FRANK C. AND CLARA CHURCHILL COLLECTION

The collection of Frank C. and Clara Churchill consists of more than 2,000 images that document reservation life at the turn of the century. From 1899 to 1909 Colonel Frank C. Churchill, a U.S. Indian Service official, and his wife Clara traveled to reservations in more than ten states

90. Cherokee baptism, 1908.
Cherokee, North Carolina. Col.
Frank C. Churchill Collection.
N26899

and federal territories, including Florida, North Carolina, Indian Territory (Oklahoma), Minnesota, Montana, Arizona, New Mexico, Utah, California, Oregon, Washington, and Alaska. Unlike many anthropologists who were then interested in documenting and preserving traditional culture, the Churchills were reformers who endeavored to illustrate the need for government policies that promoted assimilation. Although these photographs often lack in technical sophistication, they provide a distinct view of Native life both in contact and conflict with mainstream American society.

Frank C. Churchill came to the Indian Service with a background as a teacher, a co-owner of a successful garment manufacturing concern, and a banker in Lebanon, New Hampshire. Active in local politics, he had served as head of the state's Republican party. In 1899 the Department of the Interior named him a revenue inspector for the Cherokee Nation in Indian Territory. Churchill went on to review the land allotment process in Indian Territory and to monitor affairs at numerous Indian agencies and schools as an Indian inspector. Early in 1905 he received a special appointment to investigate Native schools and reindeer service in Alaska. President Theodore Roosevelt later noted that Churchill's report and recommendations had completely changed his mind about conditions in Alaska.[8] Churchill was reappointed an Indian inspector again in 1905, and he served until 1909, when he resigned due to ill health. During his nearly ten years of service he worked under the administrations of three presidents, William McKinley, Theodore Roosevelt, and William Howard Taft.[9]

Although most of the photographs in the collection are credited to Frank Churchill, his wife Clara also took many of the images. While the Churchills made some of the photographs to illustrate his reports to the secretary of the interior, they seem to have photographed people and events largely for their own interest. In a fragment of a letter to an unknown recipient, Churchill states, "My photographs are mounted in books and so classified that no one book is illustrative of the subject. I have something over 4000 pictures from about 75 tribes and remnants of tribes. Views of individuals vary widely according to education and Christianization of indians."[10] Churchill, who was not professionally trained, apparently had become familiar with photography by joining friends in making photographs of Lebanon and its environs.[11] In any case, the increasing portability of photographic equipment in the 1890s made it easier for the Churchills to document conditions in distant Indian communities.

As devout Congregationalists, the Churchills were strong proponents of evangelization (fig. 90). Churchill valued the efforts of missionaries in Native communities, noting that, "Throughout the entire indian service enthusiastic missionaries may be found and the results of their work varies according to the intelligence of the indians, and the degree of civilization which the individual has attained."[12] After Churchill's death in 1912, Clara Churchill frequently lectured to social and church groups on Indian subjects and illustrated her presentations with lantern slides made from their photographs. These presentations featured titles such as "My Indian Friends" and "Ten Years Among the Indians."[13]

Along with Christianization, Churchill believed that education was key to solving problems in Indian communities, observing, "As a race they are opposed to progress, no matter what its form, be it book knowledge, religion, industry."[14] He bemoaned the influence of Indian families, complaining that "girls graduate from school and have every appearance of education and refinement but go back to squallor [sic] and the blanket. . . . It is almost always on account of the unfortunate influences of the old home, which they cannot withstand."[15] At Hopi (fig. 91), Churchill justified forcible school attendance policies, given that "whoever trys [sic] to conduct that scholl [sic] will have to face howling mothers and grandmothers."[16] Schoolchildren were a favorite subject, and Churchill made portraits of students at many Indian schools (fig. 92).

During his tours of duty Churchill often encountered Natives forcibly removed from their traditional lands and compelled to relinquish former ways of life. People in these circumstances frequently were in desperate need of assistance for their very survival. Churchill was sent to inspect agencies troubled by complaints of fraud and mismanagement. His visit to the White Earth Agency in Minnesota was prompted by accusations that, among other issues, the local Indian agent supplied poor quality horses and domestic stock to the Chippewa in contravention of stipulated agreements. One of his photographs taken at White Earth suggests the complete authority wielded by Indian Agency officials (fig. 93). A large pile of clothing and household items heaped on the ground is identified as things to be destroyed on Churchill's order.

Churchill genuinely believed that his advocacy of policies designed to help Indians assimilate

91. Hopi basketmakers, 1903. Oraibi, Arizona. Col. Frank C. Churchill Collection. N26276

92. Pima girls peeling vegetables, 1906. U.S. Indian School, Sacaton, Arizona. Photo by Col. Frank C. Churchill. Col. Frank C. Churchill Collection. N26473

93. Condemned Ojibwe (Chippewa)
property ordered destroyed by U.S.
Indian inspector Col. Frank C.
Churchill, 1906. Wild Rice River,
Minnesota. Photo by Col. Frank C.
Churchill. Col. Frank C. Churchill
Collection. N27557

94. Peace officers traveling to the Chitto Harjo (Crazy Snake), Creek uprising, 1901. Photo by Col. Frank C. Churchill. Col. Frank C. Churchill Collection. N27092

95. Chitto Harjo (Crazy Snake), Creek, and his band, 1901. Harjo is on the far right. Muskogee, Oklahoma. Photo by Col. Frank C. Churchill. Col. Frank C. Churchill Collection. N27099

to mainstream norms in the long term would benefit Indian people, whom he largely saw in the subordinate role of children requiring firm but loving parental guidance. "The time will come when the great work now being done by the government and well-balanced missionaries will show mighty results . . . it is a work of evolution that is to bring the indian race to what we boastingly call civilization."[17] Nonetheless, he recognized that government policies, such as land allotment, had the potential to make Native people vulnerable to manipulation and abuse. Discussing the problem of white men manipulating land leases on allotments at the Osage Agency in 1903, Churchill lamented, "It is the old story over again. As soon as a way is provided for the white man to get a foothold upon Indian soil, he is bound to do it."[18]

One series of photographs Churchill made in Indian Territory (later Oklahoma) depicts the aftermath of the Indians' last organized resistance before the reservation system was consolidated. In 1901 armed federal troops were sent to suppress what was called the Crazy Snake Rebellion in Indian Territory. Chitto Harjo (whose Creek name can be translated as Crazy Snake and whose English name was Wilson Jones) was a Creek farmer, orator, and leader. He became a prominent figure in the Creek resistance to the Dawes Severalty Act, the 1887 legislation that attempted to destroy the reservation system (and thereby promote assimilation) by abolishing tribal corporate ownership of land and requiring Indians to receive allotments of 160 acres of land.[19]

Harjo believed the U.S. government was obligated to uphold the terms of the 1832 treaty that promised the Creeks would be maintained in the Indian Territory "forever" after their forced removal from traditional homelands in Alabama. A group of Creek traditionalists traveled to Washington in 1900 to lobby the government to support their position. Erroneously thinking that senior government officials had affirmed their interpretation of the 1832 treaty, Harjo and other dissident Creeks, who came to be called Snakes, set up a traditionalist government and attempted to enforce their own laws on the reservation, including threatening any Creek who accepted an allotment and instituting bans on employing and leasing land to whites. Harjo's compelling oratory attracted other Territory Indians and ultimately led to the formation of the Four Mothers Nation, one of the first intertribal groups opposed to allotment and other assimilationist policies.

Pressured by both white settlers and some Creeks, local officials appealed to Washington for troops. In January 1901 the government sent federal troops to arrest Harjo and other resisters for conspiracy, assault, and battery (fig. 94). At some point after their arrest, Churchill photographed Harjo and some of his associates, probably while they were awaiting trial (fig. 95). The pose that the men were forced to assume makes them look as if they were part of a school group portrait, rather than mature men arrested for attempting to preserve their culture from outside attack. Although the men have physically complied with the photographer's directions, their expressions reflect their despair.

The Churchills' interest in demonstrating the benefits of "civilization" largely led them to avoid taking photographs of the exotic or picturesque elements of Native culture and views of the noble or dangerous warrior. Instead, their images range from depictions of ramshackle housing to smiling schoolchildren and churchgoers. For the Churchills, the era of the Indian as "other" was over, and they were prepared to bring Native people into the fold of mainstream society.

EDWARD H. DAVIS COLLECTION

Perhaps because George Heye saw himself as a self-made archaeologist, he was drawn to maverick personalities from the time he began collecting Indian objects. Among the most independent of Heye's employees was Edward H. Davis, a transplanted easterner who took up photography and ethnography after he arrived in Mesa Grande, California, in 1885. Heye purchased Davis' collection of southern California Indian artifacts in 1915, and the next year Heye traveled to Mesa Grande to meet him. Sporadically for nearly seventeen years Davis collected objects for Heye in southern California, Arizona, New Mexico, and northern Mexico. In 1948 Heye purchased some one thousand negatives that Davis had selected to represent the best of his many years of photographing Indian people.

96. Refugio, a Kumeyaay (Diegueño) woman, burning an effigy of Judas, 1905. Mesa Grande, California. Photo by Edward H. Davis.

Born in Brooklyn, New York, Davis trained as an artist before he traveled to San Diego in 1885 to recuperate from kidney disease. (He lived to be in his late eighties.) After working as a draftsman and an architect, and successfully speculating in San Diego's booming real estate market, Davis purchased more than three hundred acres on Mesa Grande, east of San Diego, and moved his family there. Over the next several years he worked as a fruit grower, a farmer, and a cattleman, among other callings. After he sold his collection to Heye, Davis built a resort hotel called Powam Lodge, where he entertained guests with spellbinding Indian and adventure stories. The hotel burned to the ground in 1930.[20]

According to his grandson, Davis was fascinated with the local Kumeyaay (Diegueño) community known as the Mesa Grande Indians, and he soon began to collect objects from them.[21] Over time he photographed them and recorded stories and other information about their customs (figs. 96, 97). His interest in Indians eventually commanded the majority of his time and energies.[22]

Davis developed close relationships with his Kumeyaay neighbors, who made him a ceremonial chief in 1907.[23] The Kumeyaay permitted Davis to witness and photograph private religious observances such as the Eagle Dance and other rituals to commemorate the dead. They

not only allowed him to photograph these occasions, but they also requested that Davis make prints for them, including portraits of recently deceased family members. (This custom may seem strange now, but it was very much in vogue in the United States and Mexico in the nineteenth century.)[24]

After meeting Heye, Davis began to travel to Arizona and New Mexico, often by horseback, wagon, and foot, to collect specimens at Heye's direction. Evidently Davis took photographs during these expeditions (fig. 98), but he did not send them to the museum as some of Heye's other contracted collectors did. Neighbors recall seeing Davis "on a saddled horse with fifty pounds of photographic equipment on his back, heading out again and again toward the desert . . . coming back . . . after weeks or months of absence, dusty, but jubilant, with a little more of history recorded in his black box."[25]

Like many of the early independent collectors with whom Heye worked, Davis frequently traveled to isolated places where life itself, not to mention photography, could be tenuous.

In securing these photos it should be borne in mind that I had to pay my subjects for every picture and where money would do no good, in far distant mountains, I paid in thread, needles, safety pins, combs, small mirrors, face paint, also panoche, native sugar in Mexico and candy. Without things to trade I could get no photos. Not only that, but hundreds of miles on mule back on desert &

98. Tohono O'odham man gathering fruit from saguaro cactus, 1919. Near Blackwater, Arizona. Photo by Edward H. Davis. N24484

mountain trails. Nearly all Inds [sic] were suspicious, and the Yaquis dangerous and so for all these negatives I had to work for and use all the diplomacy I was capable of.[26]

Davis associated his photographic ethics with his own survival in his travels in Mexico (fig. 99).

In taking photos I always ask consent of [the] subject and pay for it in money or candy, but if they object, I never insist. I heard of 2 Americans in a car below Hermosillo, Mex [sic] and coming toward them a troop of ragged Yaquis on the warpath against Mexican militia. The Americans stopped and got out their camera to snap a photo. The Inds [sic] warned them no picture but the Americans paid no attention & proceed to take the picture, but it was never taken as 2 dead Americans were left in their auto. The reason I am alive and writing this is that I never took a photo under protest.[27]

Among Davis' most significant accomplishments were photographs and collections of objects acquired from the little-known Seri of Tiburon Island in the Gulf of California. The Seri, famous for their violent dislike of outsiders and reputed by local Mexicans to be cannibals, had been visited by Americans only once before, in 1895. Davis traveled to Tiburon Island several times, beginning with a trip in 1922, to collect for Heye and returning as late as 1936 at the age of seventy-four.

The wide variety of images Davis made during these repeated visits to Tiburon Island illustrate his eclectic intentions. While he recorded conditions essentially as he found them, Davis also tried to recapture aspects of Seri traditional culture by posing his subjects. In one case he persuaded a young Seri woman to put on a pelican-skin cloak (fig. 100), a part of Seri traditional dress before they began to wear cotton clothing. "By coaxing, wheedling and joking, Roberto [Davis' interpreter] finally persuaded a young woman to put on the Pelican kilt, and she gradually pulled off her shirt . . . and laughingly permitted it. As her brown shoulders and breasts were exposed she covered them with her arms and hands while I took the photo. I gave her some blue powder to decorate herself with and a little round mirror."[28] Issues of manipulation and sexual abuse not withstanding, this image suggests a distinctly different image of Seri women from others that Davis took, which show women with somber expressions and little exposed skin.

99. Opata men dressed (possibly as centurions) for Easter ceremony, 1922. Opodepe, Sonora, Mexico. Photo by Edward H. Davis. N24984

100. Seri woman, 1924. Tiburon Island, Sonora, Mexico. Photo by Edward H. Davis. N23814

Like Heye, Davis lived to collect, but he also seems to have had a penchant for danger and adventure. He traveled to some of the most remote tribal communities in Mexico, such as the Yaqui and Huichol, who were known for their hatred of white men. Davis described his collecting as akin to the work of a trader, but one with a mobile post.[29]

Heye seems to have met his match in Davis, a man who loved a "good deal." Years after Davis had ceased collecting for him, Heye was still trying to get Davis to donate his photographs to the museum. Heye even enlisted his friend Joseph Keppler to convince Davis to give his photographic collection to the museum, but to no avail.[30] Ultimately, Davis agreed to sell Heye a selected group of images, but not without some fierce negotiations. "If you knew the hardships I had to go through to secure these photos you would want $2 for each one. Now since you feel

I am overcharging, I would be willing to cut the price to 75¢ each and I think I have met you half way and let it go at that."[31]

In many ways Davis' images present the mystery of photography and its practitioners. Not a professional photographer, anthropologist, or government official, Davis had no visible aesthetic or didactic agenda in taking his pictures. His photographs emerge from his friendship with neighbors and his curiosity about unknown people and unfamiliar customs. He had a natural sense for intimacy in portraits and often framed his subjects dramatically. Aside from the photographs he sold to Heye many years after their creation, Davis sought no profit from his camera work.

Like most men of his time, Davis expressed contradictory ideas concerning Indians, ethics, and collecting. He professed a great respect for Indians, but he was sometimes surreptitious when collecting "sensitive" objects, such as cremated burials. On one occasion Davis arranged to meet an informant near Warner Springs to excavate several burial *ollas* at an abandoned village. When he unexpectedly encountered a group of Native men cutting wood, he was forced to wait for hours before he could retrieve the remains.[32] (These burial items were returned to the Luiseño tribe under the provisions of the Native American Graves Protection and Repatriation Act.) Despite, or perhaps because of, these conflicting impulses, Davis succeeded in expressing in his images both his own humanity and the humanity of his subjects.

FRANK G. SPECK COLLECTION

Anthropologists have played a key role in creating and defining images of Native Americans in the nineteenth and twentieth centuries. At the beginning of this century, anthropologists typically conceptualized human society as an evolutionary continuum from the primitive to the civilized, with Indians being at an earlier, more primitive stage.[33] In the interest of salvaging a "pure" representation of Native culture, many anthropologists sought to present Indians in a pristine or "traditional" condition. Government anthropologists were influenced by assimilationist policies and often created romantic images of the West that in turn may have promoted white settlement in Indian lands.[34]

Renowned anthropologist Frank G. Speck, founder of the anthropology department at the University of Pennsylvania, significantly contributed to the tradition of anthropological imaging. While Speck, like most anthropologists, used photography to document his research, he brought to it a distinctly different sensibility about Native Americans and their relationship to mainstream society.

Speck was born into a New York mercantile and seafaring family of Dutch and Mahican Indian ancestry. Plagued by ill health as a child, he was sent to live in Connecticut with family friend Fidelia Fielding, a Pequot Indian. Speck spent seven years with her in Mohegan. He left at the age of fifteen to complete high school in New Jersey after the aging Fielding could no longer care for him.

Fielding spoke and wrote Pequot fluently, had strong views on cultural preservation, and held little regard for white mainstream society.[35] Speck learned Pequot and developed a lifelong love and facility with Native languages. Through his relationship with Fielding and her family, Speck became aware of the realities and complexities of Native American culture in the modern world.

Speck pursued linguistic studies at Columbia University, and his professors, who included Franz Boas, encouraged him to study Native languages. He eventually acquired from Fielding a vast body of documents, diaries, and letters in Pequot. Tragically, these writings were destroyed in a house fire before they could be completely analyzed and processed. This calamity deeply affected Speck for many years.[36]

In 1907 Speck accepted a fellowship at the University Museum at the University of Pennsylvania, where he received his doctorate degree. He probably met George Heye around 1908, when Heye housed his collection at the University Museum and assumed an active role on the museum's board of directors. Speck never worked directly for Heye, but he did collect objects for him (as well as for several other museums) as a way to finance his field research. He formed collections for Heye for almost twenty years, from around 1910 to 1929, and he also published several books and articles through the museum's publication series.

Where and how Speck became familiar with photography is unknown. He was famed for his precise documentation and for his use of sound recording equipment in addition to still and moving cameras.[37] Ethnohistorian C. A. Weslager described the contents of Speck's field bag.

> On field trips it was stuffed with pajamas, an extra shirt, comb, and brush, notebook, and other miscellaneous articles, including a battered Kodak of ancient vintage held together with rubber bands. I once told him his camera reminded me of Oliver Holmes's "wonderful one hoss shay," and without notice it would suddenly turn into dust. "Why should I buy a new camera?" was his reply. "There's nothing wrong with this one." The joke was on me, for in some mysterious fashion it produced excellent photographs.[38]

Speck devoted his professional life to researching the Algonquian and Iroquoian peoples in the Northeast (fig. 101). He went into the field regularly whenever his university teaching schedule permitted, and on weekends he often traveled to nearby Indian communities in Virginia and Delaware. Speck pursued a comprehensive and wide-ranging Boasian research program, and he published his findings extensively. He synthesized field data and ethnohistorical research on a broad range of subjects, including language, technology, religion, music, ethnobotany, and art, in an effort to interpret and understand Native cultures in an organic and inclusive manner. Scholars consider his work on Montagnais and Naskapi hunting communities in Canada to be among his most important accomplishments (fig. 102).[39] Speck also trained several generations of anthropologists, including Frederick Johnson and Daniel Davidson.

Friends and associates of Speck widely remarked on his easy way with Native Americans and his facility with Indian languages, as well as his love of humor and practical jokes. His interest in

101. Canoeing in bark canoe, 1924.
Penobscot, Indian Island, Canada.
Photo by Frank G. Speck. N12979

102. Naskapi girl, 1924. Seven
Islands, Quebec, Canada. Photo by
Frank G. Speck. N12130

103. Salmon weir, 1919. Near
Tadousac, Quebec, Canada. Photo
by Frank G. Speck. N13028

natural history and the interrelationship of human beings and the natural world profoundly
influenced his research, and in some ways anticipated the development of ecological anthropology.[40] This intimate association with nature and with the physical world in which people live
is a distinctive element of his photographs (fig. 103).

In 1914 Speck conducted research on the mixed-blood communities in tidewater Delaware and
Virginia. Among these remnant groups in Virginia, such as the Rappahanock, the Pamunkey, and
the Mattaponi, were descendants of the mighty Powhatan Confederacy, which was first encountered by English settlers in the seventeenth century. By the beginning of the twentieth century
only small communities, sometimes just a few family groups, remained in isolated rural enclaves
near the Atlantic Coast (fig. 104). Although some intermarriage with whites and African Ameri-

104. Nanticoke boys, ca. 1911.

Delaware. Photo by Frank G. Speck.

N1278

cans had occurred in past years, Speck believed that these communities retained a tribal cultural identity.

> These racial considerations are entirely aside from the determination of their social tradition. The latter is emphatic and consistent. It is the one bond by which the various Indian communities cohere. And there is no fair basis of ethnic or historical evidence which would lead the open-minded to distrust it, unless beheld through the eyes of those bound to the deadly routine of race or class prejudice. The reason for referring to this is that the latter exists even among their neighbors.[41]

In the years that Speck conducted research in Virginia he became an advocate for the Rappahanock (fig. 105) (as he did for many of the tribes with which he worked), and he encouraged their efforts to obtain government recognition and educational benefits for their children. In 1925 the museum published Speck's monograph on the Rappahanock in the midst of a heated controversy over their claim to Indian identity. By then the Rappahanock had organized a tribal committee and presented state officials with their claim for recognition. At that time in Virginia (as well as in many other areas of the South), government policies classified any person with the slightest amount of African-American blood as "colored." To assert a "pure" Indian identity was to claim to be white.

W. A. Plecker, state registrar at the Virginia Bureau of Vital Statistics, reacted irately to the Rappahanocks' efforts to identify themselves as Indian. "As to the amount of Indian blood, where there is any, we are not prepared to say and are not particularly interested, as the new Racial Integrity law says that no person with any trace of negro blood can ever be classed as a white person or intermarry with the whites."[42] He objected to the publication of Speck's monograph and threatened the museum. Speck responded by asserting academic freedom and advocating Indian rights. "The publication of my paper in its present form will be a victory for free judgment on the CULTURE status and traditional identity of mixed Indian communities that will vitiate the endeavor to blackwash and annihilate them. . . . I refuse to betray the Rappahanocks and their kindred into the hands of an ignorant iconoclastic politician."[43]

Speck's practice of a supremely humanistic and exacting anthropology, his warm personal and professional relationships with Indian people, and his profound love of nature combined to define a distinctly different way of representing Native Americans. While Speck was generous in presenting gifts when he visited communities, he never paid for information (or, most likely, for

105. Rappahanock men hauling fish nets, 1918. Chickahominy River, Virginia. Photo by Frank G. Speck. N12638

photographs).[44] His images reflect his deep belief in the integrity and viability of Indian cultures, and his strong desire to understand their histories and their adaptations to the modern world.

THE HENDRICKS-HODGE EXPEDITION

In the early years of the twentieth century, anthropologists became increasingly interested in the question of "cultural persistence" as opposed to "cultural decline."[45] No longer content merely to "salvage" Native American material culture and images for science and posterity, anthropologists now sought to document the persistence and continuity of Indian communities. Zuni Pueblo, long isolated in western New Mexico, must have seemed the perfect laboratory for scientific inquiry. By the 1920s generations of anthropologists had traveled there to answer a host of research questions, none of which were defined by the Zunis themselves.

The Hendricks-Hodge Expedition to excavate Hawikku, and later the nearby site of Kechiba:wa, was the first large-scale project initiated after the Museum of the American Indian was officially incorporated in 1916. The expedition was named after its chief financial patron, Harmon W. Hendricks, and its director, Frederick Webb Hodge. (Hodge had left the

106. Ruins of Hawikku from the
southwest, 1920. Hendricks-Hodge
Expedition. N7205

Smithsonian Institution's Bureau of Ethnology during the course of the project to take a position at the museum.) The expedition eventually encompassed one of the largest and most systematic excavation and photographic projects in the Southwest. It also incited a fervent controversy in the Zuni community that ended in 1923 with a near riot at the Shalako dances and the confiscation of the museum's film camera by Zuni religious leaders. This traumatic event ended the outside photography of religious ceremonies at Zuni Pueblo and soured many Zunis towards the seemingly endless stream of anthropological visitors.[46]

From the beginning Zuni had inspired fantasy among Europeans and later among Americans. Hawikku (fig. 106), one of six ancestral Zuni villages occupied when Europeans arrived in the New World, is famed in historical literature as the site of the Spaniards' first encounter with Native people in the area of today's Southwest. In 1539 the Zuni at Hawikku repelled a small party of Spaniards that was searching for the fabled Seven Cities of Gold. The Spaniards were led by Fray Marcos de Niza and Esteban, a survivor of Álvar Núñez Cabeza de Vaca's ill-fated crew who had succeeded in walking from the Gulf Coast of Texas to Mexico in the 1530s. The defenders of Hawikku faced Diego de Coronado in a brief but fierce battle in 1540, but they were overpowered by Coronado's weapons, dogs, and horses. Almost one hundred years later the Spanish occupied the region and built a mission at Hawikku in 1629 to convert the Zuni to

107. Zuni workmen excavating
Hawikku, 1921. Gaialito is in Room
339 (foreground); Frederick Webb
Hodge is in the background.
Hendricks-Hodge Expedition.
N7472

108. Zuni workmen eating dinner at
Camp Harmon, 10 August 1917.
Photo by Frederick Webb Hodge.
Hendricks-Hodge Expedition.
N1959

Catholicism. After the Pueblo Revolt in 1680, which ejected the Spanish from New Mexico for twelve years, the Zuni permanently abandoned Hawikku.

Occupied for generations before Coronado's arrival, Hawikku's longevity and its singular history in the early European settlement of the New World had long intrigued archaeologists. Scholars speculate that Hodge first encountered the site when he accompanied the Smithsonian's Hemenway Expedition to Zuni in 1886. Most probably he later interested Heye and Hendricks in an archaeological excavation. After Hodge and Heye traveled to Zuni to view the site in 1915, plans for the expedition were soon under way.

With Hendricks' financial support, Heye sponsored the expedition to excavate Hawikku during six field seasons, from 1917 to 1923. Excavations in 1919 and 1923 at the nearby site of Kechiba:wa were jointly sponsored by the museum and the University Museum of Archaeology and Ethnology at Cambridge University. Under Hodge's direction a team of anthropologists, including Jesse L. Nusbaum, Edwin F. Coffin, Victor Schindler, Donald Cadzow, Samuel K. Lothrop, George H. Pepper, and Alanson Buck Skinner, worked with more than twenty Zuni to carry out the most comprehensive excavation project then undertaken in the United States (figs. 107, 108). They excavated more than 370 rooms in the village, the large mission church and friary, and more than 1,000 burials. They recovered at least 1,400 pottery vessels and hundreds of artifacts of Zuni and Spanish manufacture.

The expedition was notable in its scope and methodology. Hodge and his team employed pioneering excavation techniques such as stratigraphic chronology, a method whereby they excavated an area in sequential layers to create a visible chronological record of the site's occupation. Hodge also collected ethnographic material that was related mostly to domestic and ceremonial life at Zuni Pueblo. He hoped to establish links between ancestral and contemporary Zuni practices and to demonstrate the ongoing vitality and endurance of Zuni culture.

Although photographing the site was clearly a secondary goal of the expedition, Hodge nonetheless oversaw the creation of one of the era's most comprehensive visual records of an anthropological expedition, producing more than 1,250 negatives and 11 films. These images document the methodology and features of the excavations. They also provide portraits and record many aspects of Zuni life, such as daily activities, agriculture, craft work, and ceremonial events. Little is known about Hodge's photographic intentions at the time of the expedition. An analysis of the images does suggest that Hodge gave photographic assignments to specific expedition members (who varied from year to year). Pepper and Cadzow, for example, photographed most of the ethnographic subjects. Coffin and Lothrop concentrated on the archaeological excavations, while Nusbaum documented a mix of subjects. Many of these anthropologists had earlier collected and photographed for Heye, and it may be that Hodge and Heye identified each photographer with particular skills.

Of the scores of ethnographic photographs that resulted from this expedition, many appear to have been taken either to illustrate Hodge's ethnographic material collections—a series on

109. Zuni men harvesting wheat, 1919. Ojo Caliente, New Mexico. Photo by Jesse L. Nusbaum (?). Hendricks-Hodge Expedition. N5602

making pottery corresponds with the museum's collection of contemporary Zuni pottery—or to portray contemporary links to colonial or prehistoric practices. Photographs of grain harvesting might be compared with archaeological evidence of farming methods (fig. 109). Some images record activities rarely practiced at Zuni today, such as the stick race (fig. 110), a traditional social event held between men of different villages. In the early twentieth century many Zunis still spent the summer months in small farming villages near agricultural fields some distance from the main Pueblo. With the advent of automobiles, most reservation residents now live year-round at the Pueblo.

While the photographers on the expedition clearly strived to be documentary and scientific in their scope, the ethnographic images they produced raise intriguing questions concerning both the "accuracy" of their ethnographic reporting and their relationship to their subjects. Some photographs appear to have been staged. For example, in the series of photographs on pottery-making, the potter works on a rug under a tree with her tools and supplies around her (fig. 111). In "real" life a potter would never work on a rug for fear that the mud and dirt would spoil it. She would more likely make pottery while seated, either inside at a table or on the ground near the doorway to her home, where she could keep an eye on domestic affairs. In another series on constructing a type of outdoor adobe oven that the Zuni still use to bake bread, one of the two women building the oven wears what was probably her best traditional clothing (fig. 112). Such a

choice of apparel is highly unlikely, given that this is messy work being done in an era when many Zuni were wearing mainstream clothes. This series was taken at the expedition's Camp Harmon, rather than at the nearby Zuni farming village of Ojo Caliente or the main Pueblo, where the Zuni maintained ovens.

Why did the photographers and their subjects make these choices? Did the photographer feel that situating the potter on the rug under a tree made a better, that is, more artistic, image? Did the technical requirements of the camera make it difficult to photograph indoors? In the images of building an oven, did the photographer show some Zuni women in their traditional clothes to emphasize a cultural continuity, or did the women prefer to wear their best clothes for this photograph?

Many of the ethnographic photographs seem to depict either the Zuni workmen who labored in the excavations or members of their families. It is now impossible to know how these Zunis felt about having photographers in their community. Did they feel coerced into being photographed, or did they participate freely? The photographers might have paid their subjects or made other arrangements to compensate them. Correspondence between Heye and Hodge indicates that on at least one occasion Heye sent copies of photographs to the workers.[47] Perhaps the photographs were taken with the proviso that copies be returned to the families. By that time Zunis preferred

111. Zuni woman, smoothing the surface of a pottery jar, 1918. Hawikku, New Mexico. Photo by George H. Pepper. Hendricks-Hodge Expedition. N2271

112. Zuni women building oven, 1919. Camp Harmon, Hawikku. Photo by Jesse L. Nusbaum. Hendricks-Hodge Expedition. N4717

cash for services, and other anthropologists report paying informants and subjects.

It is known that photographing ceremonial events deeply disturbed some Zunis. Throughout the expedition Hodge took particular pains to photograph social and ceremonial events, ranging from social dances performed at Ojo Caliente, the summer farming village near the expedition camp, to annual religious dances, such as the summer Rain Dances and winter Shalako observances at Zuni Pueblo. In addition to taking still photographs, Hodge directed filmmaker Owen Cattell in the creation of some 10,000 feet of film footage (fig. 113).

Ultimately, the expedition's efforts to photograph Zuni ceremonies led to its premature end. From the beginning Heye and Hodge were aware that factional politics in the community might "inconvenience" the expedition. Writing to Hodge in 1916, Heye alluded to this potential danger by noting, "There is evidently some trouble at Zuni and all factions should feel perfectly well contented before we go in there to do any work."[48] At that time the Zuni were struggling to cope with social, educational, and agricultural regulations imposed by U.S. government policy and the local Indian agency. The community was divided in its attitudes towards these changes. Heye cultivated the support of Zuni community members and leaders, even hosting Zuni governor Waihusewa and Lorenzo Chavez when they visited New York in 1923 (fig. 114). Hodge also seems to have become involved in the community's politics. He instructed Heye to purchase silver medals (modeled after those presented to New York fire fighters) to give to Zuni

113. Owen Cattell filming Rain Dance, 1923. Zuni Pueblo, New Mexico. Hendricks-Hodge Expedition. Photo by Victor Schindler. N35853

authorities, and he interceded with the local Indian agent in disputes over land use and the operation of the local government.[49] He even ordered decorative canes for his supporters, evoking the symbolism of the ceremonial canes bestowed on the Pueblos by Abraham Lincoln. Hodge's supporters among the Zuni appear to have convinced some Zuni leaders to issue Hodge permits to photograph the ceremonies by asserting that the photography was sanctioned by authorities in Washington.[50] Since Zuni leaders were regularly required by the U.S. government to pledge allegiance to the United States, invoking this authority presumably carried much weight. Hodge also made cash contributions to particular individuals to support the dances.

Nonetheless, Cattell's attempt to film the 1923 Shalako ceremony so aroused the objections of some community members that Zuni priests confiscated his camera and film during a volatile

114. Zuni Governor Waihusewa,
Lorenzo Chavez, George Gustav
Heye, and Frederick Webb Hodge
by Grant's Tomb, 1923. New York.
Photo by Thea Heye. N21020

confrontation at the dances. The local Indian agent, R. J. Bauman, recovered the film and camera weeks later and returned them to the museum. Some Zuni families still tell stories of these events, and today the Zuni tribe does not permit photography of ceremonies on the reservation.

The museum's relationship with Zuni Pueblo did not end with the expedition's conclusion in 1923. In the 1970s the Pueblo requested that the museum cease its public distribution of films concerning religious subjects, and the museum donated a set of films to the Pueblo at that time. In 1985, more than sixty years after the expedition carried out its excavations, the National Endowment for the Humanities funded the Hendricks-Hodge Expedition Documentation Project, which brought together museum staff, Zunis, and outside scholars to document the long-neglected artifact and photograph collections and to create computer databases of the collections and excavation records to promote research and community use. Since then, the databases have made it easier to use the photographs to study pottery and to research historic Zuni seasonal farming villages.

In the spring of 1995 Rose Wyaco, a Zuni tribal member working under a NMAI fellowship, conducted a review of the photographs and the 1985 computerized database of the Hendricks-Hodge photographic collection. During this three-month project, Wyaco examined more than 1,690 photographs and compared them with the database subject categories. She identified culturally sensitive images, such as burials, dances, and religious individuals, corrected misidentified photographs, and provided additional descriptive information. In addition, she clarified the current collection inventory by identifying duplication in the negatives and vintage prints, most of which had been made from original negatives.

While the ultimate utility of these images to scholars and to the Zuni is yet to be determined, the photographs generated by the Hendricks-Hodge Expedition today find uses unimagined by Hodge's team of anthropologist-photographers. The Zuni Bilingual Education Program of the Zuni School District (the only school district in New Mexico administered by Native Americans) is integrating the photographs into their Zuni materials development process. The main objective of this process is to produce bilingual curriculum materials using culturally appropriate data. The Hendricks-Hodge collection, along with other images of Zuni, will provide a framework for developing bilingual cultural materials following selected themes. The photographs will be accompanied by new captions written from a Zuni perspective in the Zuni language.

Looking back over the more than seventy years that have passed since these photographs were made, it is easy to detect both the desire of the expedition's leaders to contribute to human knowledge and the reality that these images of Native Americans were made under the inevitably distorting conditions of life on an Indian reservation. The Hendricks-Hodge collection, despite its turbulent history, continues to provide opportunities for mutual cooperation and research between the Pueblo of Zuni and the NMAI. That Zuni tribal members and scholars today find these photographs useful and meaningful testifies to the images' transcendent qualities.

Having attended both Catholic and government boarding schools as a child, I am interested in how the experiences of Indian boarding school students compare to my own often negative memories. In 1996, I photographed students at the Sherman Indian High School in Riverside, California. Established at the turn of the century as a boarding school for Native children, the school has gone through many changes over the years. At Sherman, I was pleased to meet and photograph these students, for whom the school clearly has been a positive experience. —D.G.

115. Intertribal student government. Back, from left: Lori Estrada, Dalene Copperfield, Leah Duncan, Marsha Nez, Renee Jim, Olivia Bronco, Malia Castillo; front, from left: Doug Littlehat, Doug Jones, Teri Jones, 1996. Sherman Indian High School, Riverside, California. Photo by Dorothy Grandbois. P26523

116. Teri Carnes and Andy Meson, 1996. Sherman Indian High School, Riverside, California, Photo by Dorothy Grandbois. P26524

117. From left: Eric Lorretto, Laticia
Chavez, Eddie Dock, James Dehose,
Angelo Lewis, 1996. Sherman Indian
High School, Riverside, California.
Photo by Dorothy Grandbois.
P26525

118. Phillip Narcisco, Heyrend
Yazzie, and Alfonzo Alchesay, 1996.
Sherman Indian High School,
Riverside, California. Photo by
Dorothy Grandbois. P26526

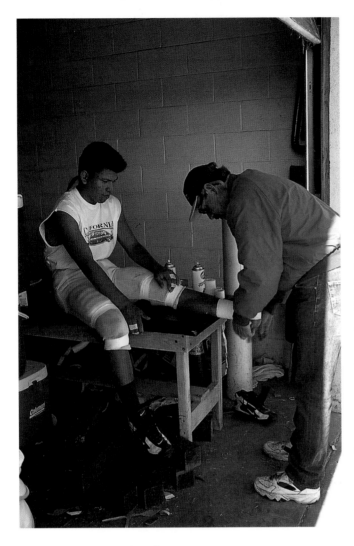

119. Lewis Bennet preparing to play football, 1996. Sherman Indian High School, Riverside, California. Photo by Dorothy Grandbois. P26527

121. Sandra Melboy and Harrison Gorman, 1996. Sherman Indian High School, Riverside, California. Photo by Dorothy Grandbois. P26528

110

120. School friends (unidentified),
1996. Sherman Indian High School,
Riverside, California. Photo by
Dorothy Grandbois. P26529

3. Processes and Pictures

*The Beginnings of
Photography and of
Photographing
American Indians*

Nigel Russell

Before the independent announcements of the invention of photography in 1839 by the Frenchman Louis Daguerre (the daguerreotype process) and the Englishman Fox Talbot (photogenic drawing), the only way western explorers could record the wondrous sights they encountered was through the efforts of a skilled artist. Explorers soon learned that the successful reception of the drawings largely depended upon the artist's talent and interpretation of the scene. Some form of drawing aid was needed that would be less fallible than the human hand or the artist's memory.

The first instrument tried was the camera obscura, a precursor to the photographic camera that had been in use since the sixteenth century. It was little more than a simple box with a lens at one end and a focusing screen at the other. This was far from a perfect solution as an artist's tool: the larger the picture required, the larger the box and lens, and the dimmer the resulting image. In addition, the image was upside-down and reversed left to right. Even with improvements, the results were far from perfect.

In 1806 William Hyde Wollaston patented the camera lucida, a small prism mounted on a telescoping rod with a clamp on the opposite end that could be attached to a drawing board. When the artist placed one eye close to the prism, he saw an image of the scene before him superimposed on the drawing board below. The camera lucida's small size and the artist's ability to see an un-reversed image in broad daylight made it the drawing instrument of choice for the artist-explorer and scientific traveler.

One of these artist-explorers was the Englishman Frederick Catherwood, who was in New York City in 1839 when news of the daguerreotype's invention reached America. He had been in New York since 1836, exhibiting large panoramas of the Holy Land that were based on camera lucida drawings he had earlier made on a trip to the Middle East. John L. Stephens, an American explorer and travel writer, suggested that the two of them explore the ancient ruins

Detail, fig. 142.

122. Daguerreotype with notation "Peter Wilson—Wa o wa wa na onk to his friend P. E. Thomas—Sa-ga-oh," ca. 1840. P24065

of Central America, the vast majority of which had not been seen by white men since the Spanish conquest. Stephens wanted to prove or disprove the popular belief that these ruins were the work of an old world civilization, most likely the Egyptians, and dated from the time of the pyramids.

Excited by the new invention of photography, Stephens sponsored D. W. Seger to give the first public lecture on the subject in America.[1] Unfortunately, Stephens' travel plans were set, and he set sail with Catherwood for Central America on 3 October 1839, two days before the lecture. With no training in photography and unable to obtain one of the few daguerreotype cameras then in the United States, Catherwood used his camera lucida for the expedition's drawings. Upon discovering the ruins of the Mayan city of Copan, Stephens negotiated their sale from a local farmer for $50. Reluctantly, they cut short their explorations when Catherwood contracted malaria in the Yucatan and returned to New York in July 1840. The camera lucida drawings formed the basis for the illustrations in Stephens' book *Incidents of Travel in Central America, Chiapas, and Yucatan* (1841). In it, he asserted that the magnificent ruins they had discovered were constructed by the descendants of the current aboriginals and dated from the time of Columbus. The detail in the drawings was so great that a century later an American archaeologist looking at pictures made at Copan in 1839 wrote that it was possible to decipher the date inscribed in hieroglyphs, even though, when Catherwood made the drawings, their meaning was still a mystery.[2]

On their second trip to the Yucatan, from October 1841 to mid-June 1842, they were accompanied by the Boston surgeon and ornithologist Dr. Samuel Cabot. They took along a daguerreotype camera and wasted no time experimenting with it upon their arrival in Merida. For practice, they offered to take portraits of the lovely young colonial ladies of the town.

Stephens, trying to excuse their inexperience, began by explaining to the sitters all the possible mistakes that can be made with the daguerreotype process (figs. 122, 125).

> I took occasion to suggest that the process was so complicated, and its success depended upon such a variety of minute circumstances, it seemed really wonderful that it ever turned out well. The plate might not be good, or not well cleaned; or the chemicals might not be of the best; or the plate might be left too long in the iodine box, or taken out too soon; or left too long in the bromine box, or taken out too soon; or a ray of light might strike it on putting it into the camera or in taking it out; or it might be left too long in the camera or taken out too soon; or too long in the mercury bath or taken out too soon; and even though all these processes were right and regular, there might be some other fault of omission or commission which we were not aware of; besides which, climate and atmosphere had great influence, and might render all of no avail.[3]

Their early efforts at photographing Native Americans were largely failures, and they turned their attention to the Mayan ruins. Stephens described their working process.

> Mr. Catherwood made minute architectural drawings of the whole, and has in his possession the materials for erecting a building exactly like it; and . . . as on our former expedition, he made all his drawings with the camera lucida, for the purpose of obtaining the utmost accuracy of proportion and detail. Besides which, we had with us a daguerreotype apparatus, the best that could be procured in New-York, with which, immediately on our arrival at Uxmal, Mr. Catherwood began taking views; but the results were not sufficiently perfect to suit his ideas. At times the projecting cornices and ornaments threw parts of the subject in shade, while others were in broad sunshine; so that, while parts were brought out well, other parts required pencil drawings to supply their defects. They gave a general idea of the character of the buildings, but would not do to put into the hands of the engraver without copying the views on paper, and introducing the defective parts, which would require more labour than that of making at once complete original drawings. He therefore completed everything with his pencil and camera lucida, while Doctor Cabot and myself took up the daguerreotype; and, in order to ensure the utmost accuracy, the daguerreotype views were placed with the drawings in the hands of the engravers for their guidance.[4]

Probably because of their inadequate experience with the process they never seemed to master photographing in the bright sunlight and extreme contrasts of light and dark encountered in Central America, but they persisted. Upon reaching a site, the Indians accompanying the expedition used their machetes to clear the overgrowth from the ruins while Stephens and Cabot readied the daguerreotype camera, and Catherwood set up his drawing board (fig. 123).[5]

They returned to New York with numerous daguerreotypes and Catherwood's drawings, which were used as guides for the 120 engravings included in Stephens' second work, *Incidents of Travel in Yucatan* (1843). This was probably the earliest published use of photographic images in the exploration of the New World.[6] Many of the engravings from Catherwood's drawings show Mayans in the foreground, and in his book Stephens often mentions the activities in which they

123. Las Monjas, Uxmal, Mexico, 1843. Drawing by F. Catherwood. Length 103.75 cm. Photo by Pam Dewey. 11.6113

are engaged. This was done, however, to add "color" and scale to the ruins, for Stephens exhibited little real interest in the area's inhabitants since they knew nothing of the history or culture of their ancestors. Tragically, all the daguerreotypes, most of the drawings, and all their Mayan artifacts, which it was hoped would form a museum, were lost when Catherwood's quarters caught fire on 31 July 1842, less than six weeks after their return to New York. Among the lost relics was the only known Mayan wooden beam carved with a glyphic inscription ever found.[7] What fire did not destroy was ultimately lost to water. Catherwood, along with the few remaining daguerreotypes and drawings, was lost to the Atlantic when his ship, the S.S. *Arctic*, collided with the S.S. *Vesta* in a heavy fog in late September 1854 and sank.

While Stephens was the first to *publish* the results of photography on an expedition in the Americas, he was preceded by Edward Anthony in the *use* of daguerreotypes as an integral part of an expedition. Anthony's trip, taken in October 1840, also marked the first U.S. government-sponsored use of documentary photography in an exploration. It was Anthony's job to photograph a range of disputed highlands on the border of northern Maine that the British claimed did not exist, even though the boundary was spelled out in the Treaty of Paris in 1783. Anthony's daguerreotypes of the highlands and boundary landmarks helped settle the disagreement and led to the Webster-Ashburton Treaty of 1842. Did Anthony also take photographs of the other members of the expedition, including the Native American guide? We will never know. The images taken on the expedition were forwarded to the State Department and subsequently lost.[8]

The earliest remaining photographs of Native Americans were not taken in America at all but in the United Kingdom. Kahkeqaquonaby (Sacred Waving Eagle's Plume; he was also known by his Christian name, the Reverend Peter Jones) was the son of a Welshman and a Mississauga woman from Ontario. He lived with the tribe until he was sixteen and later became a Methodist

124. Ojibwe Indians who toured with George Catlin, ca. 1846 (copy ca. 1900). From left: Bird of Thunder (Hannah Henry), The Great Hero (George Henry), The Elk, The Pelican, Woman of the Upper World, and the Furious Storm. Toned gelatin silver copy print. P9078

missionary to the Indians, translating several religious tracts into Chippewa. He visited Great Britain on four occasions, and sometime in late 1844 or early 1845 he was photographed by the Scottish calotypists David Octavius Hill and Robert Adamson.[9]

The calotype or talbotype was an improvement of Talbot's original photogenic drawing process. Unlike the daguerreotype, in which each image was unique, the calotype employed a negative produced on paper so multiple positive copies of the same image could be made. Even with the later improvement of waxing the paper to make it more transparent and to allow less of its texture to show in the final print, the calotype never matched the sharpness of the daguerreotype, and it was seldom used in the Americas.

George Catlin spent eight years painting western Indians and collecting eight tons of their belongings. He exhibited his paintings and artifacts in New York and Philadelphia, and tried to interest the U.S. government in purchasing his collection. Finding little interest here, he transported his vast collection to London and opened his exhibition on 1 February 1840. It was a huge success, due in part to the great interest in Native Americans generated by the best-selling novels of James Fenimore Cooper and the widely held belief that North American Indians were headed toward imminent extinction.

By the spring of 1843 Catlin was exhibiting his collection in Manchester, where he met the

American showman Arthur Rankin, who was touring with nine Ojibwe (fig. 124). One member of the troupe was Maungwudaus, who was also known as Great Hero or George Henry. (He was also the half brother of the Reverend Peter Jones, who had been photographed by Hill and Adamson.) Catlin and Rankin formed a partnership and returned to London to give a private performance for Queen Victoria. With a good deal of publicity, they reopened the exhibition with a live show of the Ojibwe performing war dances, holding a war council, smoking the peace pipe, and demonstrating an Indian ball game, played, with difficulty, indoors under gas lights.[10]

Catlin arranged daily field trips for the Ojibwe, in Native attire and face paint, to see the sights and, of course, to be seen by the public. Trips were taken to the daguerreotype studios of London. These images, made of Native Americans abroad and upon their arrival back home as celebrities, are among the earliest photographs to have survived.[11] In 1844, when the partnership dissolved, the Ojibwe were replaced, with the help of P. T. Barnum, by sixteen Ioways.

In 1842 John Charles Frémont was unsuccessful in his attempts to use a daguerreotype camera on his first expedition to the Rocky Mountains. Frémont made no mention of his photographic failure in the official government report. His experiments were not made public until 1954, when the diaries of Charles Preuss, the German artist and cartographer in the expedition party, were published. Thirteen days after heading west from Fort Laramie, Preuss wrote:

> August 2: Yesterday afternoon and this morning Frémont set up his daguerreotype to photograph the rocks; he spoiled five plates that way. Not a thing was to be seen on them. That's the way it often is with these Americans. They know everything, they can do everything, and when they are put to the test, they fail miserably.[12]

Three days later he noted: "August 5: Today he said the air up here is too thin; that is the reason his daguerreotype was a failure. Old boy, you don't understand the thing, that is it."[13]

By Colonel Frémont's fifth expedition in 1853–54, he was willing to give photography another try. He hired Solomon Numes Carvalho, a daguerreotypist and artist, to accompany the expedition. Carvalho soon realized that the other men in the party resented having to carry with them all his necessary photographic equipment.

> The packing of the apparatus was attended with considerable trouble to the muleteers, and also to the officer whose duty it was to superintend the loading and unloading of the mules; and they all wanted to be rid of the labor. Hence the persecution to which I was subjected on this account. Complaints were continually being made to Col. Frémont, during the journey, that the weights of the boxes were not equalized. Twice I picked up on the road the tin case containing my buff, &c., which had slipped off the mules, from careless packing—done purposely; for if they had not been fortunately found by me, the rest of the apparatus would have been useless.[14]

On their journey along the Arkansas River, Carvalho had his first experience photographing Native Americans.

125. Daguerreotype of Eastern Indians, with clothing ornaments accented in gold, ca. 1850. P24064

The Cheyenne village, on Big Timber, consists of about two hundred and fifty lodges, containing, probably, one thousand persons, including men, women and children. I went into the village to take daguerreotype views of their lodges, and succeeded in obtaining likenesses of an Indian princess—a very aged woman, with a papoose, in a cradle or basket, and several of the chiefs. I had great difficulty in getting them to sit still, or even to submit to have themselves daguerreotyped. I made a picture, first, of their lodges, which I showed them. I then made one of the old woman and papoose. When they saw it, they thought I was a "supernatural being;" and, before I left camp, they were satisfied I was more than human.[15]

During the winter, the expedition suffered great hardships. Frostbitten and hungry, Carvalho buried his camera and equipment in the snow to hide it from the Indians in the hope of someday returning to it. He never did. In 1856 Frémont became the Republican candidate for president, and he never finished his report on the expedition. Most of Carvalho's daguerreotypes may have been lost in 1881 when the warehouse in which the Frémonts stored much of the material for the unfinished report caught fire. All that remains of the photographs taken on that expedition is one badly damaged daguerreotype of an Indian village in the collection of the Library of Congress.

John Mix Stanley, a daguerreotypist and a well-known painter of Native Americans, was taking Indian portraits at Fort Gibson in Arkansas Territory as early as 1842. In the spring of 1853 Stanley joined Isaac I. Stevens, governor of the Washington Territory, on an expedition to survey a possible northern railroad route to the West Coast. Stevens wrote in the expedition's official report that on 4 September at Fort Benton,

> Mr. Stanley commenced taking daguerreotypes of the Indians with his apparatus. They are delighted and astonished to see their likenesses produced by the direct action of the sun, and they consider Mr. Stanley was inspired by their divinity and he thus became in their eyes a great medicine man.[16]

What became of Stanley's daguerreotypes is not known. Perhaps they perished in 1865 when a fire at the Smithsonian destroyed many of Stanley's Indian paintings.

The 1850s witnessed great changes in the evolution of photography. The daguerreotype process reached the height of its popularity at the beginning of the decade (fig. 125). It was reported that 403,626 daguerreotypes had been taken in the Commonwealth of Massachusetts alone in 1854, the overwhelming majority of which would have been portraits.[17] By the end of the decade the taking of daguerreotypes had faded to almost nothing.

126. Ambrotype of Chief Okemos (Ojibwe [Chippewa], b. ca. 1780, d. December 1886), a nephew of Pontiac, 1858. Sheboygen, Michigan. Photo by Henry H. Smith. Gift of Mr. Joseph Imhof. P12521

127. Tintype of Mohawk youths, ca. 1890. Rye Beach, Rye, New York. P23470

In 1851 Frederick Scott Archer, an Englishman, published a workable alternative to the paper negatives used in the calotype. His process, which became known as the collodion or wet-plate process, used glass plates coated with a solution of collodion and potassium iodide that were then sensitized in a silver nitrate bath. After coating, individual plates were exposed in the camera when the collodion had begun to set but before it was dry. They were promptly developed, fixed, and washed.

Three years later, in 1854, James Ambrose Cutting of Boston patented the ambrotype process. After a glass wet-plate negative was exposed, it was processed in such a way that, when mounted with a piece of black cloth or paper, it gave the appearance of a positive. Like the daguerreotype, the resulting one-of-a-kind image was usually placed in a small decorated leather or thermoplastic case (fig. 126).

Hannibal L. Smith, a professor at Kenyon College in Ohio, patented his melainotype process two years after the introduction of the ambrotype. His process later became known as the ferrotype or, more commonly, the tintype (fig. 127). Like the ambrotype, each image was unique, but a tintype was unbreakable and less expensive and quicker to produce. Instead of a photograph on glass backed with a black material, the image was exposed directly on a thin sheet of black varnished iron. While it never reached the high level of popularity that the ambrotype achieved in 1856–57, the tintype remained in use at seaside resorts and by itinerant street photographers for more than a century.

Albumen printing paper, also introduced in the early 1850s, hastened the demise of the earlier calotype paper process as well as the use of daguerreotypes and ambrotypes. An unlimited number of prints could be made from a single wet-plate negative, and the resulting images had a sharpness and a warm brown tone that was far superior to any previous paper photograph. Paper coated with a mixture of egg white (albumen) and salt was sensitized by floating the coated side in a bath of silver nitrate. The paper was then hung in the dark to dry. To make a print, the paper was placed in a frame in contact with the negative and exposed to sunlight until the image appeared. After exposure, the print was toned a "sepia" color with gold chloride, fixed, and washed. Such contact printing required the glass negative to be the same size as the final print. To capture the majesty of the West's scenic wonders, photographers struggled with cameras that used glass plates as large as 20 by 24 inches.

All government-sponsored expeditions, which were then under the supervision of the Corps of Topographical Engineers, a separate branch of the War Department, ceased during the Civil War. After the war, however, a new breed of professional photographer headed west. These men were full-time photographers, many of whom had gained their expertise by photographing battle scenes or taking carte-de-visite portraits of soldiers for their loved ones back home.

One of these men was Ridgeway Glover, who recounted his adventures in a series of letters to the *Philadelphia Photographer* magazine and served as a special correspondent for *Leslie's Illustrated Weekly Magazine*. He photographed the Brulé and Oglala Lakota near Fort Laramie in late June 1866 but complained that he could print less than half of his fifty negatives because "the water was so muddy." A month later he wrote from Fort Phil Kearney in Montana Territory that "I am surrounded by beautiful scenery, and hemmed in by yelling savages."[18] He was unsuccessful in obtaining "instantaneous views" of an encounter with some Cheyennes. "My collodion was too hot, and my bath too full of alcohol, to get any pictures of them, though I tried hard. They attacked our train in the rear, killed two of the privates, and lost two of their number."[19] In August he commented that while he was taken by the scenery, he had failed to make many good negatives. The next report in the *Philadelphia Photographer* was an editorial note that "Mr. Ridgeway Glover was killed near Fort Phil Kearney on the 14th of September by the Sioux Indians. He and a companion had left the Fort to take some views. They were found scalped, killed, and horribly mutilated."[20]

Although he had set up a portrait studio in Omaha in 1867, William Henry Jackson preferred the outdoors, and a year later he was making trips to photograph the surrounding area (figs. 128, 129).

There were other picturesque things also to lure me afield. Several Indian reservations—Pawnees, Omahas, Winnebagoes, and Poncas on the north, Otoes and Osages on the south—were within a

128. Carte de visite of
Noosadedentcoom (White Horse),
a Pawnee scout, ca. 1868–69. Photo
by William H. Jackson. Donated by
Miss Laura Havemeyer. P20548

129. Blue Hawk and Coming
Around the Herd (Pawnee), ca.
1868–69. Photo by William H.
Jackson. P18686

hundred miles of Omaha. Many friendly Indians of these tribes I had met in the city. I had even prevailed upon some of them to come into the gallery and pose for their pictures. It was no unusual sight to have the reception room filled with groups of blanketed squaws, papooses, and bucks, willing for a small recompense to brave the "bad medicine" of the camera. The result was many interesting portraits of the red men; but I was anxious to photograph them in their native settings.

A traveling outfit had to be devised to enable me to take photographs of the outlying scenes. . . . The pioneer photographer of that time had to be something of a chemist as well as an artist, and a mechanic also. He had to carry with him a kind of laboratory with many chemicals, trays, glasses, and other apparatus, for each plate must be prepared on the spot for every exposure. . . .

My first outfit for field work was . . . a dark room on wheels, built on the back part of the running gears of a light buggy, minus the springs, and was drawn by a single horse. Inside it was fitted with a sink, a tank for water, and other conveniences for picture making. This was a handy, if

130. Stereoscopic albumen print of
Naskapi (?) woman, ca. 1870. David
C. Vernon Collection. Presented by
Laurance S. Rockefeller. P21509

primitive, outfit, and with it I traveled over much of the prairie country north of Omaha, principally to get the Indian in his own home. The Pawnees, the most interesting of all, were living in permanent villages of earthen lodges, but there were also many tepees, so it was not hard to find good photographic subjects.[21]

Andrew Joseph Russell was the official photographer of the Union Pacific Railroad. In one of the letters he sent back to Nunda, New York, he describes his experiences photographing an Indian settlement near the Weber River.

> I set up the instrument, took the picture, made a failure as they supposed that I could take them whether they stood still or not. The second attempt was a success. . . . It made a unique group. There were no two dressed alike. . . . The squaws were dressed and painted for the pictures [also]. . . . What pleased them most was that I got the papooses . . . and as they recognized each others' faces. . . . They believe that when their picture is taken, that white man see what they are doing no matter where they are. . . . They were after me to-day to take [a] picture of [the] white man that stole a gun from one of the tribe. They said you take his picture, we catch um.[22]

With the mass production of photographs now feasible, stereoscopic photography, introduced in the early 1850s, began to increase in popularity (fig. 130). When two photographs, taken just inches apart, were viewed in an optical device called a stereoscope, the resulting image appeared in three dimensions. Stereoscopic photographs became so popular that by the early 1870s the majority of photographs taken of Native Americans in that period were in stereo

131. Hopi women, ca. 1871. Photo by
Edward O. Beaman. Presented by
Frederick S. Dellenbaugh. P10654

format. Stereo views of Native American subjects, however, never sold as well as scenic views of the West. It is estimated that 2,000 to 2,500 stereographs of Indian subjects were published before 1885, compared to 12,000 to 15,000 views of California, of which more than one-third were of Yosemite and the giant redwoods.[23]

When Edward O. Beaman photographed Native American cities in the desert of Arizona (fig. 131), he took along a friend, two mules, items to trade with the Indians, and enough glass plates for one hundred stereoscopic negatives. Writing in 1872, he describes what must have been a typical outfit for an intinerant "stereographer."

> For an outfit of one hundred 5 × 8 negatives I require three boxes of about the following dimensions: eight inches wide by fourteen deep and eighteen long. In one I carry my camera, instruments and about thirty plates for immediate use; in another my bath and chemicals for working with, and in the remaining one my stock of glass, etc. These boxes, with leather straps around them, make a very easy pack to fasten on an animal; by hanging them on the pack saddles, and covering over with a dark tent, blankets, etc., and then throwing the diamond hitch around them in the packer's style, a mule will carry them all day without the least danger of breakage.[24]

Photographers in Washington, D.C., had a much easier time—they simply waited for the Indians to come to them (figs. 132–134). The practice of photographing visiting delegations began as early as 1852, when nineteen Arapaho, Cheyenne, Lakota (Sioux), Oto, and Iowa traveled to Washington after signing the Fort Laramie Treaty of September 1851. The number of diplomatic trips increased so much that more than ninety delegates representing thirteen tribes visited Washington in the winter of 1857–58. In 1859, Joseph Henry, the first secretary of the Smithsonian, suggested that the government commission photographs of these delegations rather than purchase images from professional studios. After the 1865 fire that destroyed the Smithsonian's paintings of Indians by Stanley and Charles Bird King, Henry again requested funds to institute a more systematic way to assemble "a far more authentic and trustworthy collection of likenesses of the principal tribes of the U.S. . . . The Indians are passing away so rapidly that but few years remain, within which this can be done and the loss will be irretrievable and so felt when they are gone. The photographs . . . should be single and of what is known as imperial size, . . . [and] the pictures should be portraits of the men and not of their garments or ornaments."[25]

132. Delegates from the Yankton, Santee, Upper Missouri Sioux, Sac and Fox, Ojibwe, Ottawa, Kickapoo, and Miami tribes posing with President Johnson on the steps of the White House, 23 February 1867. The handwriting identifying figures on the balcony is that of Gen. W. Tecumseh Sherman. Photo by Alexander Gardner, Washington, D.C. Presented by P. Tecumseh Sherman in 1932. P10142

133. Dakota delegation to Washington, D.C., 1875. P22365

134. Oto delegation to Washington, D.C., January 1881. Photo by John K. Hillers. (seated from left) Standing Eating, Baptiste Deroin, and Harikara (Standing Buck); (standing from left) Crawfish Maker, and James Arkeketah (?). P3408

Henry's request was refused, but the trade in commercial photographs of Native Americans continued to grow.

While the wet-plate negative printed on albumen paper reigned as the standard photographic process from the 1860s to the late 1880s, a number of improvements gradually took photography out of the exclusive domain of professionals and made it available to a growing number of amateurs. The first advancement was the introduction of gelatin dry-plates. Although the process had been suggested by Dr. Richard Leach Maddox in 1871, commercially manufactured dry-plates were not available to photographers until the end of the decade. Photographers could now pack a camera and enough glass dry-plates for a day's work and then develop them at leisure in the evening. If that was not feasible, a darkroom tent could be brought along in which to develop the negatives on the spot.

Gelatin-coated silver bromide printing paper next appeared on the market. More sensitive to light than albumen paper, this "gas-light" paper could be exposed to a negative indoors, under artificial light, and the image could be chemically developed in a short time. The paper's increased sensitivity also made it truly practical to enlarge small negatives. Professional photographers proved reluctant to give up familiar processes, and paper coated with the newer gelatin-silver emulsions did not replace albumen paper until the early 1890s.

135. Gelatin silver print of
Alompum and Tax-a-lax (Cayuse),
twin grandnieces of Chief Joseph,
b. February 1898. Photo by Lee
Moorhouse, 2 October 1898. P10361

136. Gelatin silver print of
Alompum and Tax-a-lax (Cayuse),
twin grandnieces of Chief Joseph,
b. February 1898. Photo by Lee
Moorhouse, 2 October 1898. P10362

137. Lantern slide of Eskimo (Inuit) summer seal-hunting encampment with inflated sealskins, July 1899. Plover Bay, Siberia. Photo by Edward S. Curtis. Gelatin silver on glass. Harriman Alaska Expedition. N21480

Typical of this new class of enthusiastic amateur photographer was Major Lee Moorhouse, who photographed Northwest tribes at the turn of the century (figs. 135, 136). Even though camera equipment had changed, many of his experiences were the same as those of photographers fifty years earlier. Much like his predecessors, he made the same mistake of generalizing the behavior of one individual being photographed as being indicative of the attitudes of an entire tribe or even all Native Americans.

There are instances among the Indians where the prejudice against the camera is too deep-seated to be overcome by friendship or money. The superstitious fear it inspires in these is not to be toyed with. For instance, I tried to get one of the most prominent Indians in the North-West to sit for me a short time ago, but he flatly refused. For 25 years I had known him and enjoyed his confidence. He was getting old, was somewhat enfeebled, and as much of the very life-threads of Northwest history were woven by him and his forefathers I was particularly anxious to secure a good negative of him. Love, money and persuasion failed.

A young Indian who had just returned from school and who had listened to the conversation between this obdurate old fellow and myself said to me, "You know why Five Crows no want his picture took?"

I replied, "No, Red Elk, why is it?"

"Five Crows think if he has picture took, he go to hell sure," was the astonishing reply. But many of the Indian tribes have caught the white man's touch of vanity and some few of the old fellows and many, many of the younger generation can be seen loitering around the studios, admiring the photographs of friends who, dressed in their gaudiest robes and ornaments, had submitted to a sitting for the artist. After an old Indian once gets the photographic fever, and is encouraged by an artist in whom he has confidence, the old fellow will take pride in arraying himself in all the tribal regalia and ornamentation at hand and will sit a dozen times a day. But this specimen is very scarce.[26]

With the widespread use of gelatin dry-plates in the 1890s, lantern slide projectors evolved from the "magic lantern" of parlor entertainment into a classroom tool used to illustrate art, history, and science lectures in the universities (fig. 137). After 35mm cameras became popular in the 1930s, these large 3¼ by 4-inch black-and-white glass slides were replaced by the smaller and lighter 2 by 2-inch cardboard mounted color transparencies still in use today.

The most significant improvement to photography in the late nineteenth century was the invention of a way to coat a transparent flexible film base with a gelatin-silver emulsion. Early

138. Filming totem poles, ca. 1910. Northwest Coast. P24011

139. Cree and Stoney Indians, 1926. Saskatoon Fair Grounds, Saskatoon, Canada. Panoramic gelatin silver print. Photo by Gibson Photo. Presented by Kenneth C. Miller. P11462

experiments with rolls of sensitized paper had met with only limited success. William Henry Jackson tried some newly marketed "Sensitive Negative Tissue supplied in bands for Roller Dark Slide" on his 1877 trip to the Southwest to photograph the Moqui pueblos and the ruins at Chaco Canyon. He developed the occasional negative successfully in field, but upon his return to Washington, D.C., he developed the paper rolls, only to find all 400 exposures were blank. Jackson theorized that "the most costly setback of my career" was caused by the latent images fading away due to the long time between exposure and development.

Hannibal Williston Goodwin, an Episcopal minister from New Jersey, filed a patent application on 2 May 1887 for his new process of adhering an emulsion to a flexible film base. Two

140. Portrait of Apache chief James
A. Garfield. The Detroit
Photographic Company, 1899.
P22466

141. Tissue proof of photogravure of
Calf Child (Blackfoot) from Edward
S. Curtis' *The North American Indian*,
Volume XVIII, 1926. Plate #641

years later George Eastman used the superior celluloid film to replace the sensitized paper rolls
in his recently developed Kodak camera. Even a novice could operate this small "hand camera"
that was preloaded with a roll of 100 exposures. When all the pictures were taken, the whole
camera was sent back to the Eastman factory, where it was loaded with fresh film and returned
with the 100 finished prints from the previous roll (see fig. 185).

Contrary to the trend towards roll-film cameras, Lee Moorhouse preferred to use a folding
dry-plate camera. In practice, he found the new Kodak had a distinct disadvantage.

Indians have a greater horror of the small kodak than of the large camera. If an artist wants to find
serious trouble, all he need do is to take a small kodak and go among the Indians in their camp,
snapping promiscuously at tepees and Indians without permission. He will soon be informed that
his presence is not desired. They can grasp the possibility of something wonderful being confined in
a large "box," but that an equally wonderful thing could be inclosed in a pocket kodak is beyond
their comprehension and its presence at once arouses their superstition.[27]

Ultimately, transparent celluloid roll-film proved to be the perfect material that enabled photographers to capture motion on film. Within six years after the introduction of photographic film, the

first movie cameras made their appearance.

The introduction of gelatin-coated plates, film, and paper, together with developments in motion pictures, x-rays, panoramic, and early color photography, changed the way photographs were made (figs. 138, 139). Different forms of photomechanical printing dramatically altered the way photographs were seen. Through the half-tone process, which allowed text and images to be inexpensively printed at the same time, photographic illustrations could be mass-produced in books, magazines, and daily newspapers.

This influx of relatively inexpensive photomechanical reproductions made it easier for amateurs to acquire the scenes they wanted and more difficult for professional photographers, such as William Henry Jackson, to operate profitable studios. In 1898 Jackson entered into a partnership with the Detroit Photographic Company to produce and sell colored photomechanical views based upon his inventory of 10,000 negatives. The Photochrom process, a type of photolithographic printing that incorporated numerous colored lithographic stencils, enabled the company to produce inexpensive, lifelike color views at a rate of 200 prints per hour. At its height, the Detroit Photographic Company produced seven million prints per year (fig. 140).

142. Chief White Quiver, Piegan (Blackfeet) addressing his council, ca. 1912. Glacier National Park. Photo by Roland W. Reed. Toned gelatin silver print. P22456

Edward Sheriff Curtis chose photogravure, a more expensive photomechanical process, for the illustrations in his magnum opus *The North American Indian: Being a series of volumes picturing and describing the Indians of the United States, the Dominion of Canada and Alaska*. This monumental work was published in a limited edition of only 272 completed sets between 1907 and 1930, and contained more than 1,500 small photogravures illustrating the twenty volumes of text and an additional 700 large photogravures in twenty portfolios (fig. 141).

Like Catlin eighty years before, Curtis believed that the North American Indian was a vanishing race and that time was running out to photograph and catalog all the known tribes before they were overrun by the white man. Financed by J. Pierpont Morgan, Curtis set out in 1906 with an entourage that rivaled the government expeditions of earlier years.

The field season of 1906 was nine months long, beginning in the mountains of Apacheland, with snow still in sight, and long before the season ended we were snow bound in the mountainland of the Walapai. The field party for the season was, firstly, Justo, our Mexican cook; two helpers, who could best be called ethnologists, collecting the lore, logic and history of the people, one of whom acted as my stenographer—and myself, I doing the photography. . . . Our camp equipment weighed

143. Albumen print of Nez Percé men. One image (right) has been copied using tungsten light, and the other using ultraviolet light. P2914

from a thousand pounds to a ton, depending upon distance from a source of supplies; in photographic and other equipment there were several 6½ X 8½ cameras, a motion-picture machine, phonograph for recording songs, a typewriter, a trunk of reference books, . . . tents, bedding, our foods, saddles, cooking outfit, four to eight horses—such was the outfit.[28]

Just as Carvalho had struggled with his daguerreotype apparatus in the winter of 1853, Curtis had his share of tribulations.

At another time a stubborn driver rushed his four-horse team down a bank and into a freshet torrent, where, in the fragment of a minute all you could see of that wagon was its canvas top, and a muddy stream for a quarter of a mile was strewn with the wreckage. From a half dozen cameras scarcely one could be patched up out of that wreck; and plates—well, the shortest time to get a new supply was ten days and a trip to cost hundreds of dollars. Another day the pack mule with my only camera fastened to his back slipped and rolled down the canyon a mile. The camera was spread out on the mountain side seeming nothing but fragments. Twelve hours of steady, patient work and it was patched up so it could be used. But such a sight! No camera worker ever before saw anything

144. Jicaque man looking at a Leica manual, 1938. Honduras. Photo by Victor Wolfgang von Hagan. P14768

quite its equal. On the outside it was a bunch of ropes bound and twisted in every direction to hold it together.[29]

Another photographer working at this time and with an aesthetic similar to that of Curtis was Roland Reed. In the early 1890s Reed took Indian portraits, which were then sold to railroad companies whose lines crossed the West. These images became publicity photographs to prove to settlers and tourists that the West was no longer filled with "hostile" Natives but was instead an area of breathtaking scenery and colorful Indians (fig. 142). Working with a large-format camera, Reed meticulously posed his subjects in costumes and settings that romanticized an idyllic lifestyle before the days of the reservations.

Further advances in photography occurred in the early decades of this century, such as the use of ultraviolet or infrared radiation (fig. 143a, b). Sound was added to the motion-picture camera and "talkies" were introduced in 1929, but the amount and size of the equipment necessary to produce sound on film was prohibitive. Not until after World War II did it become practical for individuals to make sound movies in the field.

In 1925 the German-made Leica 35mm camera was introduced. While it was not the first still camera designed to utilize 35mm movie film, it was the first to gain favor with photographers and it greatly popularized the "miniature" image format. This small, precision-made camera offered high-quality interchangeable lenses and numerous accessories, which evolved into the "system" camera that could be adapted to photograph a wide variety of subjects (fig. 144).

The first truly practical color film—Kodachrome 16mm movie film—was made available in 1935. A year later Kodachrome slides were introduced for 35mm cameras. That format has become one of the most popular in use today (see fig. 64).

The photography of Edward Curtis now might be considered overly romantic as it perpetuates the myth of the "noble savage." Despite this criticism, Curtis is arguably the greatest of the Indian photographers. He knew what few before him or since have realized.

Each tribe or village is like unto no other, but all have their full share of superstition and secretiveness, to say nothing of stubbornness. Each tribe visited is a new situation to be taken up and mastered, and that quickly. Every phase of their life must be noted and, as far as possible, pictured, and the gathering of this lore, logic and myth must go hand-in-hand with the picturemaking, as without the knowledge of their life, ceremony, domestic, political and religious, one cannot do the picture work well.[30]

*Photographs by
Larry Gus*

145. Sign for slot machines,
November 1996. Taos Pueblo, New
Mexico. P26521

146. Cities of Gold Casino, November 1996, Pojoaque Pueblo, New Mexico. The buffalo sculpture is by George Rivera (Pojoaque Pueblo), lieutenant governor of the tribe. P26520

147. Taos Slot Room, November 1996. Taos Pueblo, New Mexico. P26519

4. Developed Identities

Seeing the Stereotypes and Beyond

Richard W. Hill, Sr.

I was looking through a stack of old postcards at a local flea market in search of stereotypical images of Indians that I might use in my university class. There were plenty to choose from: cards of Pueblo Indians performing the Eagle Dance; Navajo Indians sitting in front of their weaving looms; colorful Plains Indians mounted on horseback; Great Lakes Indians dancing at a powwow; Seminole Indians sewing their colorful clothing. Then I came across a hand-colored photo card of "Chief Cornplanter and Wigwam, Allegany [*sic*] State Park, N.Y." If I had not known who Cornplanter actually was, I would have assumed that he was a Plains Indian. He stands in front of a painted tipi, wears a feathered war bonnet, holds a peace pipe, and raises his left hand as if communicating through sign language. This little postcard represents centuries of stereotypical images of Indians, but what most intrigued me was the realization that even Indians began to live up to such stereotypes.

The scene in the Cornplanter postcard matches both the kind of image of Indians that might be held by tourists and the kind of cultural clichés that predominate American popular culture. Edward Cornplanter was one of many Iroquois Indians who performed for the public, usually by telling stories, demonstrating crafts, and singing and dancing. He traveled in his own version of a big top tent show, billing it as a "Double Show—Indian and Minstrel Concert" (see fig. 43). When I first began to attend the traditional ceremonies in the longhouses of the Iroquois, I was amazed to see that in the ritual dances some men wore this style of Plains clothing. The lead dancers wore war bonnets rather than the Iroquois-style headdress. Ironically, many Iroquois Indians from upstate New York had participated in the Wild West shows and adopted the dress of the Plains Indians, partly because it is very impressive, but mostly because such clothing was ingrained in the way many Americans envisioned Indians. It brought the "dress-up" Natives a good income by playing Indian.

That Plains Indian stereotype was so deeply ingrained in both Indian and non-Indian images

Detail fig. 158.

148. Hiawatha performance given by the Iroquois of the Cattaraugus reservation, New York, 1906. Photo by F. E. Moore. Presented by Reginald Pelham Bolton. N35320

that Iroquois performers, reenacting a drama of their sacred history, wore Plains Indian head-dresses while depicting ancient Iroquois in the story of the formation of their Confederacy of Peace (fig. 148). This performance, held in 1906 at the Cattaraugus Seneca reservation, south of Buffalo, New York, shows the legendary Peacemaker being heralded by the assembled chiefs. Their clothing, moccasins, beadwork, and headdresses were influenced by what they had seen in the Wild West shows that had passed through the area. This "Hiawatha" performance toured across the United States and went overseas as well.

The Plains Indian culture had become the superculture against which all Indians were measured. As a result of the famous battles in the West and the perpetuation of those images through Hollywood, all Indians were assumed to live in tipis, ride horses, wear full-feathered headdresses, and be experts at Native crafts. Comic books, toys, games, television programs, movies, and county fairs perpetuated these images. For over a century the war bonnet remained an essential part of these public representations of Indians. In the 1800s the popular notion was that the only good Indian was a dead Indian. By the twentieth century, however, it was commonly believed that the only good Indian was a dancing Indian. To survive, many Indians latched on to these stereotypes. Many Natives joined in as the larger society toyed with Indian images. To the outsider this all looked authentic; to the Indians it was just a show. It did not seem to matter that these displays perpetuated distorted images of Native culture.

In nearly every toy store in America, multicolored "Indian" headdresses, rubber tomahawks, and plastic bows and arrows are on the shelves. Through these things children absorb and literally buy into national stereotypes of Indians. During the Civil War brass bands became popular on Iroquois reservations. By the 1890s these bands played all over the countryside, bringing together a strange juxtaposition of images. Indians in war bonnets marched as they played peppy tunes on their cornets, trumpets, trombones, and drums. They wore a stylized "Indian" outfit of feathered bonnets and cloth shirts with fringe across the front, beaded belts, and collars. Seeing old photos of these bands and watching their modern-day counterparts play, I cannot help but wonder just how the Iroquois and the general public came to adopt and accept such images.

THE EMERGENCE OF THE PHOTOGRAPHED STEREOTYPE

The invention of photography in the mid-nineteenth century introduced a new dimension to Native stereotyping. Indians became collaborators, captured for eternity in strange poses that were not always of their own making. Staged poses for the camera resulted in photographs that lacked cultural depth. They were unreal. Photography brought the wild Indian into the safe confines of the home, and in doing so tamed the savage beast. These Indians might have strange costumes and surroundings, but they never appear threatening. Instead, they are enveloped in a romantic stillness and removed in time.

One enduring stereotype is that of the stoic stare of the silent savage. The slowness of early photographic technology contributed to much of this. People had to sit still, and smiling was taboo for everyone, not just Indians. Nevertheless, the sternness seen in many Indian faces has been translated as stoicism. It could just as easily be a sign of the sitter's annoyance with the pose.

Photography came into use during a time of great turmoil for Indians. The camera witnessed the implementation of the whites' Manifest Destiny and their hope to subjugate the Indians. Photography permitted editorial comments about this demise. The Indian, posed in "traditional" clothing with feathers, beads, and bones, and shown holding a weapon, embodies a cultural contradiction. Those attributes represent the past, yet the soulful gaze into the soft light seems to question the future. Until the Native American Citizenship Act of 1924, this was the

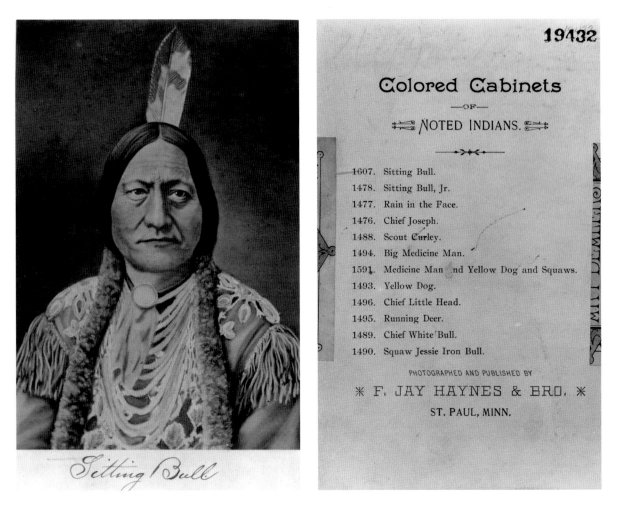

19432

Colored Cabinets
—OF—
NOTED INDIANS.

1607. Sitting Bull.
1478. Sitting Bull, Jr.
1477. Rain in the Face.
1476. Chief Joseph.
1488. Scout Curley.
1494. Big Medicine Man.
1591. Medicine Man and Yellow Dog and Squaws.
1493. Yellow Dog.
1496. Chief Little Head.
1495. Running Deer.
1489. Chief White Bull.
1490. Squaw Jessie Iron Bull.

PHOTOGRAPHED AND PUBLISHED BY
✳ F. JAY HAYNES & BRO. ✳
ST. PAUL, MINN.

149. Tatanka Yotanka (Sitting Bull), Hunkpapa Lakota, as depicted on a postcard in the NMAI Photo Archive. P19432

dominant image of Indians created by non-Indian photographers. They were icons of the battle to win the West. They were the enemy, the victims, and the prisoners of that long war.

It is difficult at best to look beyond the surface of a photograph to comprehend what was going on in the lives of the Indians who are now momentarily frozen in time. Undoubtedly some photographs were more a white man's fantasy than Indian reality. Lives of Native Americans have changed dramatically since the invention of photography, yet we are left to wonder whether these archival photographs are stereotypical images or true reflections of reality.

In most cases, these photographs "document" Indians as they lived, worked, and played in their communities. Only by peeling back the veneer created by false notions of Indians can we appreciate what was actually happening in the image. Past tendencies were to look at such photos either as factual records that preserve information on aboriginal lifeways or as evidence of cultural decay. To see beyond those two extremes, it is important to remember that different stereotypical notions about Indians are at work.

150. Tatanka Yotanka (Sitting Bull), Hunkpapa Lakota, 1882. Photo by R. L. Kelley. N21584 (P6911)

One stereotype that predominates is that of the warring chief or chanting medicine man. Male leaders often gained notoriety through their confrontations with settlers or soldiers, or through their depictions of possessing dangerous spiritual powers. Among the most famous, or perhaps infamous, Indians today are Osceola, Tatanka Yotanka (Sitting Bull), Ta-Sunko-Witko (Crazy Horse), Mahpina Luta (Red Cloud), Goyathlay (Geronimo), Cochise, and Heinmot Toolalakeet (Chief Joseph). Through photography these "wild savages" have been subdued and remade into icons of fighting Indians.

Sitting Bull's victory over George Custer at the Little Bighorn monumentalized the name of this holy man of the Hunkpapa Dakota. His image is etched in our collective memory, and photographs of him perpetuate notions about the sternness of Indians. Perhaps he wanted to be seen this way. He might well have collaborated with photographers to make himself seem larger than life. White bureaucrats also wanted photos of Sitting Bull, but primarily so military officers could identify these Indian troublemakers in the field. Ironically, Crazy Horse, the man who actually led the warriors at the Little Bighorn, refused to have his photograph taken, while Sitting Bull apparently expressed few objections.

A hand-painted image of Sitting Bull (fig. 149) is part of a larger set of postcards in the NMAI's Photo Archive. This portrait could hardly be called a stereotype, for there was no stronger Indian nationalist than Sitting Bull. Nevertheless, it is intriguing that his image became so popular among the very people he fought against. Major General O. Howard, himself an Indian fighter, represented the thoughts of many when he described Sitting Bull in 1908 as "a famous brave and a cruel, bad Indian," who had influence over the other chiefs because "they had a strange fear of medicine-men."[1] Sitting Bull's naturally creased face was considered grim, and even proof of his supposedly angry personality. Many Indians have furrowed brows that give the impression of sternness, which sometimes is misinterpreted as an indication of their determination to resist the whites. Such is the face of Sitting Bull. He never smiles in photographs, so we assume that he was quiet, brooding, and fierce. Compared to his appearance in a photograph (fig. 150), his retouched image on the postcard shows his face softened to make it seem less stern. This image was created as a tribute to Sitting Bull.

151. Red Cloud (Oglala Lakota),
1880. Photo by Charles M. Bell.
N20762 (P3586)

152. Red Cloud (Oglala Lakota), 8
December 1876. Nebraska. Photo by
Stanley J. Morrow. Presented by
Maj. Sherman Miles and Mrs.
Samuel Reber. P6964

Even though he was feared, hated, and ultimately assassinated, Sitting Bull became a proud emblem for both Indians and non-Indians. Major General Howard greatly despised Sitting Bull and labeled him a "coward," yet others called him a hero. Strangely, some whites admired him, an attitude fostered no doubt by his stint in Buffalo Bill's Wild West Show in 1865. Imagine fighting the U.S. army one year, and then touring the country to reenact those battles as a form of entertainment a few years later. Somehow Sitting Bull's struggle for his people and his homeland had been transformed into the idea that he was a noble and powerful Indian chief. The popularity of photographs of such Indians grew so rapidly that photographers began to copyright their pictures to protect their business interests.

Red Cloud, an Oglala, was another famous Indian whose reputation was transformed from that of a fierce war leader to an Indian celebrity who defended Native rights at a lecture given at the Cooper Institute in New York City. Famous for defeating the U.S. army, Red Cloud used his military victories to retain the Black Hills and to secure a peace treaty in 1868 that forced the army to abandon its forts along the Bozeman Trail. He became a real hero to his own people and something of a nobleman to many whites.

Photographed as if he were some kind of Indian royalty, Red Cloud (fig. 151) appears as a

153. Red Cloud (Oglala Lakota).

P21933

Shirt Wearer, a position of high esteem among his own people. This photo, taken by C. M. Bell in 1880, was made during one of Red Cloud's ten trips to Washington, D.C. He holds a white man's cane rather than a tomahawk or a peace pipe, perhaps to suggest his desire to blend the two cultures. The juxtaposition of the war shirt with its hair locks against the melodramatic fake rock and painted backdrop makes this a metaphorical portrait of the tamed, noble savage who has been made safe by a treaty, yet still retains his dignity. Unlike Sitting Bull or Crazy Horse, Red Cloud lived to become an example of pacification, a negotiator of change, and an advocate for assimilation in the areas of religion and education. How did his own people see him? Given a camera, would they have depicted him this same way? Was he a hero to them, or did his compromises turn him into an Uncle Tomahawk?

In a second photo (fig. 152), Red Cloud sits in front of a frame house, not a tipi, on the reservation. He looks less noble in his regular reservation clothing. Red Cloud still conveys a strong personal presence, but reservation life seems to be wearing thin on him. His was the first generation among his people forced to make the transition from the buffalo days to the reservation days. While this portrait accurately reflects Red Cloud's everyday appearance, the fabricated image of him in the studio is more widely known because it "reads" more clearly that he is an Indian chief. Such stereotypes are maintained not for any perverse racial prejudice but because preconceived ideas are so profoundly ingrained into our thinking. Images that do not meet our expectations disturb our sense of reality. People do not seem to be Indians unless they match our ideas of appropriate dress and appearance.

A later photograph of Red Cloud shows him towards the end of his life (fig. 153). Wrinkles are set deep into his face and he wears dark glasses. Once again he appears in his sacred shirt, this time with a presidential peace medal around his neck. He no longer sits tall and proud, but instead seems more pensive and downcast. It is difficult to judge these leaders who have made tremendous decisions and suffered the consequences. With this in mind, we nevertheless expect old Indians to be noble in appearance and melancholy in attitude. In this manifestation of the vanishing Indian stereotype, Native Americans face an uncertain future as white civilization advances westward.

REDRESSING THE WILD INDIAN

Wearing traditional clothing remains an important way to express communal identity. Many Indians today refer to old photographs for design ideas for their own clothing or for models for

154. Chief Frank Logan (Onondaga) and children, 1888. Photo by DeCost Smith. N22318

their artwork about "the good old days." These historic photographs, however, cannot be read too literally. One example is a portrait taken in 1888 of an Onondaga man (perhaps Chief Frank Logan) and two young girls (fig. 154). Typical of so many archival photos, this image is not in sharp focus, the subjects are stiffly posed, and no indication of surrounding events is given. The real question is, where did the man get the idea to pose in the leggings and Plains-style headdress, while his daughters wear everyday clothing? This is certainly not an expression of Pan-Indianism—the Huron, Iroquois, Micmac, Ojibwe, and other Great Lakes Indians were wearing stand-up feather headdresses long before the Plains Indians adopted the style in the early nineteenth century. Such forms of dress were introduced into other areas mainly through the influence of Wild West shows, which featured reenactments of battles fought by the Northern Plains Indians. These shows often employed Natives from other regions to play the Indian roles. Performers then took their Plains-style clothing back to their areas. In distant communities wearing these forms of dress became a way for Native Americans to express their "Indianness."

In one obviously staged photograph, anthropologist Frances Densmore sits near Mountain Chief, a Blackfeet elder, as he interprets in sign language a song that she has recorded (fig. 155). Mountain Chief was almost certainly asked to dress in his "Indian" clothing on this occasion. The bow and arrow were purposely set next to the recorder to underscore the contrast in technologies and races. The scene was arranged out-of-doors so there would be sufficient light to take the photograph. Most likely, none of this would have taken place during the actual process of translating the song. Considering this, the photo has little anthropological value other than to demonstrate how intrusive scientific inquiry can be.

Sign language was developed among the Plains Indians, whose many different dialects and languages made communication difficult at best. Still in use among the oldest Plains people today, such sign language has become a cultural cliché largely due to movies that utilized hand signals to animate the grunts of actors playing Indians. In a movie still from *Susannah of the Mounties* (1939) (fig. 156), a young Shirley Temple is dressed as an Indian and learns sign language from a Blackfeet Indian named Turtle. The first "moving" picture made by Thomas Edison in 1892 featured documentary footage of the Sioux Ghost Dance. Even though Indians were no longer considered a military threat after the massacre at Wounded Knee in 1890, movie producers kept the image of the warrior alive for decades.

155. Frances Densmore and
Mountain Chief (Blackfeet),
listening to a cylinder recording,
1916. Mountain Chief is apparently
interpreting a song in sign language.
It is possible that the cylinder
recordings were gathered by Walter
McClintock in Montana in 1898,
including words that Mountain
Chief had recorded. Photo by
Harris and Ewing, Washington, D.C.
Charles Hofman Collection. P19125

156. Turtle (Blackfeet) and Shirley
Temple in a still from the motion
picture *Susannah of the Mounties*, (1939).
P13714

157. A Wild West show sham battle, Munich, Germany, 1891. N36522 (P10210)

INDIANS AS ENTERTAINMENT

Wild West shows brought the drama of the white man's war with the Indians to audiences around the globe. One photo of a sham battle was taken in 1891 (fig. 157), one year after the massacre at Wounded Knee. What makes this blurry photo so unusual is that it was taken in Munich, Germany. Amid the dead and dying, a warrior wearing a dance bustle brings his rifle down upon a wounded soldier. The Indians were played by actual Native Americans, but little attention was paid to cultural or historical accuracy. Providing exciting entertainment and fulfilling stereotypes were among the show's primary objectives.

Another scene seems to be a photo drama unto itself (fig. 158). Standing in front of what appears to be stage scenery, a dour-looking Long Wolf holds a pistol on his equally glum wife.[2] Only the expression of the baby, who happily smiles at the camera, belies the seriousness of the situation. Perhaps these Indians were just having their family portrait taken. Through the influence of the popular Wild West shows, Indians began to strike the stereotypical poses as they associated with those performances. It is an aboriginal form of "mugging" for the camera.

In a photograph taken at the forty-fifth anniversary of the Battle of the Little Bighorn, a Cheyenne named Porcupine plays the role of "the fallen foe" (fig. 159). Annual gatherings to

158. Long Wolf (Oglala Lakota) and his family, probably 1886. Photo by Anderson, New York. N34442

commemorate what was the greatest U.S. military defeat in its time turned the site into a national tourist spot by the early twentieth century. The area remains a popular tourist destination in Montana, and in recent years Indians lobbied successfully to change its name from the Custer Battlefield Monument to Little Bighorn National Monument. Some venerate the place as the heroic last stand of outnumbered soldiers, as in the movie *They Died With Their Boots On* (1941). Others see it as the site of the Indians' heroic victory to defend their freedom in their own land. Such duality fills Indian history and complicates the contradictory nature of stereotypes about Indians.

Hollywood created its own versions of Indian adventures, and television brought the western into American homes. Tonto, as the faithful companion of the Lone Ranger, became the most famous Indian of his generation. Today, many Native Americans criticize the fictionalized character of Tonto, yet nothing had generated more positive feelings towards Indians since John Smith's account of Pocahontas. On television Tonto was played by Jay Silverheels, a Mohawk actor who provided the only positive media image of Indians at that time. Interestingly, Tonto did not wear a war bonnet, swing a tomahawk, or scalp anyone. He spoke broken English, but he usually got the Lone Ranger out of trouble. He was a "good" Indian.

This fascination with Indians has turned into a multimillion-dollar industry centered on cultural tourism in the Southwest, the Northern Plains, and the Northwest Coast. It has also

159. Porcupine (Cheyenne) in the 45th-anniversary re-creation of the Battle of Little Bighorn, 1921. N32230

160. (opposite page) Piegan (Blackfeet) horsemen, 1912, entitled *The Landmark*. Photo by Roland W. Reed. P22455

created an economic reason to perpetuate the Plains Indian prototype. People have come to expect Indians to look a certain way, and many Natives willingly delivered that stereotype as long as they made money at it. This is why stereotypes are so deeply ingrained into both American and Indian popular culture.

The Blackfeet came to symbolize the type of Indians that tourists wanted to see. Two photographs of Blackfeet, taken around 1912, illustrate the kind of advertising art that played upon romanticized notions about the Plains Indians (fig. 160; see fig. 142). These photos were taken by Roland Reed for a book entitled *Blackfeet Tales of Glacier National Park*, which was meant to re-create the carefree life of bygone days. In one, White Quiver addresses Lazy Boy, Fish Wolf Robe, and Two Guns White Calf, among others. Their stiff poses in this sparse setting suggest these are staged images.

Winhold Reiss, a German artist who immigrated to America primarily to paint Indians in the West, made the Blackfeet popular through his artwork. Inspired by the German author Karl May and the American novelist James Fenimore Cooper, Reiss went out in search for "noble savages." On his first trip to Browning, Montana, Reiss befriended a Blackfoot Indian named Turtle. Reiss made a drawing of him in 1919, which started him on his artistic mission. "What finer thing could one do for these brave fine people, who are rapidly disappearing, than to go out to their reservations, live with them, study them and preserve their wonderful features and types?"[3]

The very first Indian Reiss ever met was Yellow Elk, a Blackfoot Indian and down-and-out

circus performer who was riding a Manhattan elevated train in 1917. Reiss took Yellow Elk to the American Museum of Natural History, where he talked the curators into allowing Yellow Elk to dress in a Lakota beaded shirt so Reiss could paint his first "real" Indian. Ten years later, in 1927, the Great Northern Railroad, which operated several hotels in Glacier Park, Montana, hired Reiss to paint portraits of the Blackfeet Indians who were employed at or lived near the park. These paintings were then used as the basis of posters and calendars to promote the park.

Reiss broke with tradition by depicting the Blackfeet as he found them. He painted many portraits of them in their everyday clothing, which made them look more like cowboys than Indians. Not surprisingly, only staged photographs and his paintings of colorfully dressed Indians were used for the park's promotional and advertising campaigns. By this time many Blackfeet had stopped wearing their traditional outfits—the Great Northern had to pay Indians to make and wear them for the sake of the tourists.

Dancing Blackfeet Indians in beautiful war bonnets of eagle feathers and magnificent outfits of bright white leathers, colorful beaded strips, and white ermine tails greeted trains loaded with visitors as they pulled into the park's railway station. It made for quite an impressive sight. It would be unfair to say that these Indians eking out a living at the park were consciously promoting stereotypes. These stereotypes already existed in the minds of the tourists. The Blackfeet just gloriously epitomized what the tourists had come to expect. It is far less appealing to compare these idealized images of the entertaining Blackfeet to the harsh reality of life on the reservation. This romanticized image of Indians became so popular that Reiss set up an art school at Glacier and taught others how to make portraits of Blackfeet and Flathead Indians.

Calvin Last Star, one of the Blackfeet dancers at Glacier, recalled that they would invite tourists to join in their round dance. "We had a little program for the tourists at 8 o'clock every night. . . . The tourists would mostly ask you to take pictures with them. . . . I think my father and the older people enjoyed it. . . . It was just something to do that was enjoyable during the summer."[4]

Some Blackfeet objected that entertaining tourists was degrading. Others complained that those Indians who did work there often made up stories and were treated like noble chiefs, even though few actually were. The railroad made them "chiefs" so they would be more appealing to the tourists, and many Indians went along with the sham. Some even asked for money before they would pose, a practice that continues today.

A similar story can be told of Banff, Alberta, where tourists flocked to experience the majestic Canadian Rockies, to be entertained by Blood Indians, and to soak up the medicinal powers attributed to the hot springs. Such cultural tourism had earlier been promoted by railroads in the southwest United States. The Santa Fe Railroad advertised that a "trip back in time" awaited anyone who boarded the "Chief" and headed to Santa Fe, Taos, Gallup, or the Grand Canyon. To attract tourists to the Southwest, some promotional photographs showed the way trains were greeted as they rolled into small stops in "Indian Country" (fig. 161). In this photo, Navajo men dressed like Plains Indians perform a hoop dance as tourists eagerly watch from their train cars.

162. Santo Domingo Pueblo man selling pottery in front of the Fred Harvey Company Indian Building at the Alvarado Hotel, 1907. Albuquerque, New Mexico. Photo by Col. Frank C. Churchill. Col. Frank C. Churchill Collection. N26672

163. Nettamu (Ojibwe), a medicine man. P20766

At some stops, tourists took side trips to Indian reservations or purchased pottery, weavings, dolls, and jewelry from Indians set up by the railroad in the hotels along the way (fig. 162).

Performing for tourists has become an Indian tradition. Professional dance troupes and performers at cultural festivals provide some insight into diverse Indian cultures, but often crowds of onlookers gather just to see the colorful Indians dance. "Medicine Man Nettamu in costume" typifies how Indians thought whites wanted to see and photograph Indians (fig. 163). Posing for the camera (another Indian tradition), Nettamu, an Ojibwe Indian, wears a buffalo-horn head-dress and shakes a "medicine" rattle. He dances in front of a tipi from which hangs a

164. Arapaho (?) boy with gun.

N36557

curlyheaded doll in a cradleboard. This hodge-podge of images makes it difficult to judge Net-tamu too harshly. For many Indians from the turn of the century to the 1950s, the economic reality was that dancing was the only way to gain respect and money. Concerns over cultural purity, artistic integrity, and the long-term effects of stereotyping were outweighed by tourist dollars.

INDIAN AS PERPETUAL WARRIOR

Where there are dancing Indians, warriors must be near by. Perhaps the image of the warrior is the most pervasive stereotype of Natives. It appears in toys, games, films, books, and in logos of sports teams. This powerful image is a difficult stereotype to assess. Admittedly, most Indians herald their warriors. To fight and kill the enemy often brought prestige and honor to Indian warriors among their own people. In fact, much of the modern-day powwow celebrates warriors, and dances are performed to recall their exploits.

Photos present different aspects of this warrior stereotype. In one photograph a warrior with a pistol in hand poses in a photo studio to cater to one stereotype (fig. 164). (He is listed as an Arapaho, but I think he is a Crow Indian.) Hundreds of such photos demystify Indian warriors by making them safe through phony poses and fake scenery. This image almost mocks the reality of the fabled warrior. Such photos were intended to illustrate a universal melodrama that exists only in the viewer's mind, one created by reading about James Fenimore Cooper's Indians, Longfellow's Hiawatha, and the fall of Custer, and by watching too many westerns on television and in movie theaters.

In contrast, a 1924 photograph of a real Yaqui fighter with bandoliers of bullets strapped across his chest (fig. 165) does not immediately read as an Indian warrior. Instead, he might be

165. Yaqui man with bandoliers, 1924. Potam, Sonora, Mexico. Photo by Edward H. Davis. N24432

interpreted as a "Mexican" revolutionary. This photo was taken a year after the death of Pancho Villa, who had led the insurrection in Mexico. An Indian himself, Villa had fought for the liberation of Indians who were considered "peasants." We often stop thinking of Indians as warriors after the massacre at Wounded Knee, which is viewed as the end of the Indian Wars, yet conflicts continued well into the twentieth century, particularly in Mexico and in Central and South America. Even today when Indians rise up against their oppressors, they are labeled revolutionaries, radicals, insurgents, militants, or terrorists. This photo and countless other images in circulation still paint Indians as rebellious people.

Compare these two photos with that of Goyathlay (Geronimo) and other Chiricahua Apache "prisoners of war" (see fig. 177) as they rested by the side of the transport train that was taking them from Fort Sam Houston, Texas, to prison at Fort Marion, Florida. This 1886 photo of the Apaches, with three armed and smiling soldiers standing guard over them, creates a powerful statement about Indians. Goyathlay was one of the U.S. army's most feared enemies. Yet here, the Apaches wear pants, shirts, vests, boots, and hats much like their white counterparts. Their clothing does not suggest that they were defending an exotic or even slightly different way of life. The faces of the Apaches do not express defeat. They do not appear defiant, but instead are resigned to the fact that they fought long and hard for themselves, their families, their land, and their heritage. Without guns, they still seem strong. Ironically, this photo was taken not too long after they had surrendered and had agreed to board a train heading east, which they thought would reunite them with their wives in Florida. When they arrived, the Apaches were imprisoned instead. In that sense, the soldiers' smiles are the most telling aspect of this photo.

A photo of San Carlos Apache scouts attests to the internal split that has always existed among Indians (fig. 166). Not all Indians look alike, live alike, or think alike. Many people hang on to stereotypes about Indians being an idealized people who live in harmony, peace, and unity. These Apaches led the U.S. army against Goyathlay, and the government used photographs of these scouts as visual propaganda to reinforce their policies.

Other rare photos of Goyathlay and his followers taken shortly before they were transported show the Indians still actively fighting. (Some of the same faces appear in both photographs.) By 1886 the struggle had taken its toll: his group numbered only thirty-five men and eighty women. He surrendered around the age of fifty-seven so the remaining Chiricahua would survive. Goyathlay spent the next twenty-three years in exile in Florida and Oklahoma. This legendary warrior was known to pose for photographs that he then sold to tourists as he presented himself at fairs, festivals, and exhibitions around the country.

166. San Carlos Apache scouts.
Photo by J. C. Burges. Gen. Nelson
A. Miles Collection. Presented by
Maj. Sherman Miles and Mrs.
Samuel Reber. P6963

When I see these photos, I can hear the voice of Allan Houser, the famed Apache artist who
passed away not long ago. He used to enthrall me with his stories about his grandfather, an
Apache who rode with Geronimo. Houser's tales brought the flight for freedom alive for me and
made Goyathlay less of an abstract icon. The tone of his voice introduced a sense of reality to
those glorious and tragic days of the Apache.

INDIAN AS NAKED APE

Most of us would prefer to see photographs of Indians wearing their buckskins decorated with
colorful beads, quills, and feathers. That is what makes them Indian. The NMAI archive contains
hundreds of photos of the "undressed" Indian wearing everyday street clothes like that of the
whites. Many members of the Indian delegations that visited Washington wore their street
clothes, dressing up only for formal presentations and official portraits.

Sometimes straightforward photos were taken for scientific purposes. Physical anthropologists
wanted to record facial types in an effort to develop a catalogue of measurements for each tribal
group, much like a visual genetic database. Two photographs of Ada Brenninger, a twelve-year-
old Ojibwe, were taken around the turn of the century (figs. 167, 168). During that time, social
scientists believed that racial determinants of intelligence were based upon the size of the skull
and brain. They also hoped to define the physical characteristics that made Indians a separate
race and to look at the ancient origins of Native cultures. Many Indian skulls and remains were
collected—some from the bodies of Indians killed in conflicts with the army—and sent to
Washington for study. This "crania study" became the leading rationalization for museums and

167. Ada Brenninger (Ojibwe, 1892–1918). Haskell Institute, Lawrence, Kansas. Frederick Starr Collection. N15369

168. Ada Brenninger (Ojibwe, 1892–1918). Haskell Institute, Lawrence, Kansas. Frederick Starr Collection. N15368

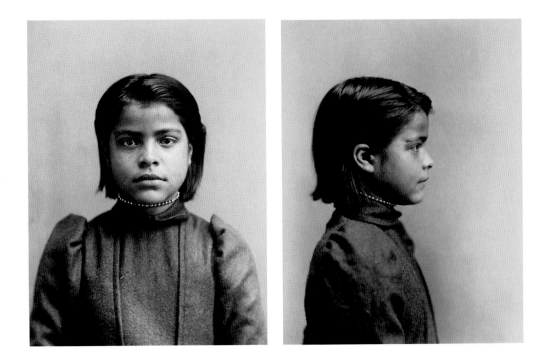

universities to collect Indian remains. It also represents a different kind of racial stereotyping. Under "social Darwinism," Asians, Africans, and Indians became the objects of study, and a hierarchy of races was formed, with people of color at the bottom of the intellectual ladder and Caucasians at the top. Many photos of Indians were used to document genetic features and to illustrate how bloodlines were either maintained or "contaminated" due to interracial breeding.

Numerous photographs were taken of Indians of whom we know virtually nothing. One photo has stuck in my mind since I first saw it in 1972 (fig. 169). It is a simple photo of a Mandan Indian named Estapoosta (Running Face) that was taken around 1874. He wears his white man's costume, but two long braids hang down on each side of his head. Large braids cover his ears while narrow braids strung with brass beads hang from his temples. I am not exactly sure what has attracted me to this photo all these years, but it has something to do with the fact that despite his clothing, his hair became the expression of his identity. This portrait made me want to grow my hair long, too.

Much later I discovered this photo's significance. Running Face was one of the few Mandan who lived through the disastrous smallpox epidemic of 1837. Only 150 survived the disease that swept through Indian Country several times. Now when I study his face, I cannot help but wonder what his eyes have seen. I find a trace of loss, but also a slight toughness that covers up his dreadful memories. To me, the stereotype represented by this photo is the story that lies behind the image. Think for a moment about the Gulf War veterans who complain of recurring health problems that they feel derive from their service overseas. The military refuses to identify the

169. Estapoosta (Running Face),
Mandan, son of Chief Red Cow,
1874. Photo by Charles M. Bell.
N34936

cause, which might be the Iraqis' use of chemical weapons. Now think what it must have been like for Running Face to watch his friends and relatives die of smallpox. What a burden it would be to bear knowing that smallpox was spread among the Indians through the distribution of blankets infected with the disease.[5]

Two other photographs that are especially important to me are daguerreotypes from the Civil War era. One shows Adrian Caesar, a Wampanoag woman, holding a baby (fig. 170). She wears

170. Adrian Caesar (Wampanoag). Herring Pond, near Plymouth, Massachusetts. N6535

171. James Mye (Mashpee). Cape Cod, Massachusetts. N6537

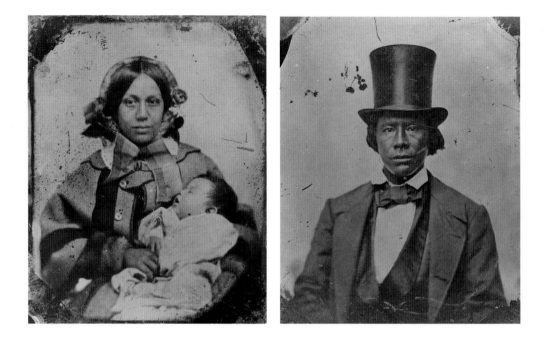

fashionable clothing and seems to be at peace with the idea of having her photograph taken. Living in Plymouth, Massachusetts, she is a descendant of the Indians who saved the Pilgrims at Plymouth Rock. History books seem to have left her behind, for very little is said about the Wampanoag after the seventeenth century. Although they did not disappear, they struggled to survive in small enclaves surrounded by a new multiracial world.

The second portrait is of James Mye, a Mashpee Indian from Cape Cod (fig. 171). The Mashpee were the object of a similar historical myopia. Part of the problem has been the American attitude toward race. Many of the Indians in New England were sold into slavery, decimated by war, and killed by disease. Scores became racially mixed with Indian, white, and African blood and were often viewed with disdain by both whites and Indians. Even today, some Indians in the West do not consider the Wampanoag or Mashpee Indians at all. They are now wrongfully judged by the tone of their skin, the texture of their hair, or the state of their lifestyle.

True, they have suffered a great deal, have sacrificed more than other Indians can imagine, and have lost much of their land base, their native language, and their traditional practices. I have spent some time among the Wampanoag and Mashpee, the Narragansett, and the Mohican, and I have to say that they remain Indians in their hearts. Their inherent "Indianness" is conveyed through the eyes of Adrian Caesar and James Mye. An untold history fills their faces. They may not be dressed like Indians, but the baby represents the hope of the Indians' future in New England. When we see a Plains Indian wear a top hat, we find it charming. When we see an Eastern Indian wear one, we assume he is the victim of acculturation. This form of stereotyping keeps us from seeing the real people in the photographs.

*Photographs by
Katherine Fogden*

This project began as a way to document the religious diversity of Akwesasne ("Where the Partridge Drums"), a Mohawk community of 8,500 people established in 1752 and located near the borders of New York, Quebec, and Ontario. Also known as the St. Regis Mohawk Reserve, Akwesasne is part of the Haudenosaunee Confederacy—Iroquois or Six Nations. Akwesasne counts among its inhabitants members of many different faiths, including the longhouse tradition, which many residents view as a way of life. A new community longhouse, in which the official business of the Mohawk Nation will be conducted, was moved to its present location at Akwesasne in 1994. These photographs reveal a community of richly diverse people bound by culture, history, family, and Native tradition.—K.F.

172. Back, left to right: Judy Swamp (Kaneratoronkwas), Jake Swamp (Tekaronianeken). Front, left to right: Logan Swamp (Ariwiio), Frank Jeremy Phillips (Aniataratison), Mason Taylor Phillips (Kaienkwironkie). Jake, a traditional longhouse spiritual leader, and his wife Judy in their home with their grandsons Ariwiio, Aniataratison, and Kaienkwironkie. Jake and Judy feel that it is very important for grandparents to ensure the future of their people by instilling their beliefs and traditions in their grandchildren. Photo by Katherine Fogden. P26530

173. Back, left to right: Juanita Snyder, James Snyder, Joe Snyder. Middle, left to right: Lorna Francis, Joe King. Front, left to right: Danielle Gibson, Nathan Francis, Cecilia Mitchell, Andy King. Cecilia Mitchell with her family on the back porch of her bakery in the village of St. Regis, overlooking the St. Lawrence River. Cecilia is a member of the longhouse. She is a traditional healer and medicine woman who gathers and prepares all her own materials. She is involved in many activities and projects that support and promote the people at Akwesasne. Photo by Katherine Fogden. P26531

174. Cecilia Mitchell visits with her son Joe Snyder in their family-owned bakery. Photo by Katherine Fogden. P26532

175. Akwesasne Mohawk Choir
members. Front, left to right:
Mildred White, Harriet Lafrance,
Akwiratehka Sharrow (infant), and
Theresa Sharrow (mother). Back,
left to right: Mary Bova, Carol Ross,
Taylor Bova, Sally Ann Adams. The
Akwesasne Mohawk Choir sings
from a hymnal that was translated
and published in the Mohawk
language in the late 1800s. The choir,
which sings each week for the
Sunday church service, is often asked
to sing at the homes of congre-
gation members who have passed on,
as part of the traditional grieving
process. Photo by Katherine Fogden.
P26533

176. Charles Lazare (standing at right) and Elaine Cook (seated at desk). Charles Lazare is in the church rectory obtaining a birth certificate from Elaine Cook, the delegated trustee of all official records at the Catholic Church of St. John Francis Regis, which has been serving the Mohawks of the St. Regis Akwesasne Community since 1752. Photo by Katherine Fogden. P26534

5. Spirit Capture

Observations of
an Encounter

Linda Poolaw

As I was growing up on the Southern Plains in Oklahoma during the 1940s and 1950s, I knew that I was an Indian. I really can't remember when I became aware of the color of my hair, eyes, or skin, but I knew that I was different from most of my classmates. In those early childhood years it seemed that the Indian kids ate and dressed a little differently, and we certainly had a lot more fun than the rest of the kids. Our folks talked in terms of "us" and "them," and we had to behave when we were in their stores and homes. Even in my early memories we always referred to the white folks as "them."

The only part of my childhood that was unique among my peers in the mixed community of Anadarko, Oklahoma, was that my dad took photographs.[1] At that time no one realized that Horace Poolaw was one of the earliest Native photographers in history, nor did anyone care. I know my three brothers and I didn't. My dad actually began making photographs in the early 1920s. My oldest brother and his mother were then living with my grandparents in the Kiowa tribal community of Mt. View, Oklahoma. Located about thirty miles east of Mt. View, Anadarko served as the agency of the Kiowa, Comanche, Apache, Ft. Sill Apache, Delaware, Caddo, and Wichita tribes of southwest Oklahoma.

During my dad's early years in photography he witnessed many ideal events, such as when his elder sister and his grandmother participated in the Ghost Dance. He took only a few shots in respect of the religious rites, but he did not know that the U.S. government had already planned to make this the final enactment of this ceremony. On those rare occasions he was able to record a group of innocent people tenaciously clinging to what was left of their identity. It will never be known if that was the moment when my father chose to become a photographer, but not until fifty years later, when his eyesight began to fail due to diabetes, did he put down his camera.

Only on rare occasions did my father allow us to travel with him on various photo sessions. When I did get to go, it was usually to help with the equipment, but for the most part I stood

Detail fig. 177.

177. Goyathlay (Geronimo), Chiricahua Apache, (third from right, front row) in front of train taking Chiricahua Apache group from Fort Sam Houston, Texas, to Fort Marion, Florida, 1886. Photo by A. J. McDonald (?). Naiche, son of Cochise, is on his right. Near Nueces River, Texas. Gen. Nelson A. Miles Collection. Presented by Maj. Sherman Miles and Mrs. Samuel Reber. P7009

behind him and watched him work. He would meticulously place people in as perfect a setting as possible, then he took ever so long to make just one or two exposures. Years later I finally realized that he took such special pains because he didn't have the means to use expensive film. His few exposures had to be perfect. I, if anybody, know of my father's impatience, but I would see him patiently work on a subject so long that it would test everyone's patience. Not until a half-century later did I comprehend that his stoic patience paid off and his work had made a real contribution to documenting Indian transitional history.

It has been written and stated repeatedly that Indian people do not like to have their photographs taken for fear of spirit capture or becoming immortal. While it might have been true in certain instances, generally my father said that he was never refused a picture, and he had enough sense not to take a picture during certain ceremonies or rituals.

When we, as Indians, venture through our past by viewing early photographs, we probably look at the faces, apparel, and settings to seek some recognition or link to kinship that is long gone. We minutely study every detail of earrings, hairstyles, necklaces, beadwork designs, and featherwork. As I search through these early photographs, I wonder just what the subjects would say to me, and I to them, if we were able to converse if only for a minute.

178. Seminole woman sewing,

Florida. P14116

178. Seminole woman sewing,
Florida. P14116

As I look through my father's collection of more than 2,000 images and rummage through photographs at the National Museum of the American Indian, I pretend that I can speak with the men and women who look back at me. I ask Geronimo how it happened that he shed his traditional clothing and now appears in a suit coat and military boots on his way to prison in Florida (fig. 177). Does he know that he is not going to meet his wife and children, that he was only told that so he would go peacefully? I wonder if the train ride across half the continent was an adventure or a punishment? Was he allowed to sing his songs of medicine to help his people in prison? Did he concentrate on his past to keep from thinking about his future? I tell him that he will survive his incarceration, that he will live as a farmer and will die a great chief in Oklahoma.

I think of Florida and of Indians in the Southeast when I look at a photograph of an elegantly dressed woman sewing patchwork on a modern sewing machine (fig. 178). I examine the neckwear and hairstyle of one woman. I wonder how her people developed such intricate patterns that are unique to the Seminole. We talk, and I tell her that my maternal great-grandmother was a Seminole taken to Oklahoma on the Trail of Tears. I softly tell her both the Oklahoma and Florida Seminoles seem to be all right in spite of the many hardships they endured. She smiles and returns to her sewing.

I stop at a photograph of eleven Native children posed for a government school photograph (fig. 179). Despite their stoic expressions and stiff postures, their shorn hair and ill-fitting uniforms make them look uncomfortable, and they look defiantly back at the camera. Were they taken from their mothers' arms and sent away to a distant school where they were beaten if they spoke in a Native tongue (fig. 180)? Did they know it would be years before many of them

179. Chiricahua Apaches upon arrival at the Carlisle Indian School, Carlisle, Pennsylvania, from Fort Marion, Florida, 4 November 1886. Photo by John N. Choate. Gen. Nelson A. Miles Collection. Presented by Maj. Sherman Miles and Mrs. Samuel Reber. P6848 (N36022)

180. Chiricahua Apache students at the Carlisle Indian School, Carlisle, Pennsylvania, December 1886. Photo by John N. Choate. Gen. Nelson A. Miles Collection. Presented by Maj. Sherman Miles and Mrs. Samuel Reber. P6847

181. Mr. and Mrs. Andrew Joe
(Mi'kmaq), 1931. Conne River
Reserve, Newfoundland, Canada.
Photo by Frederick Johnson.
N20277

would see their families again? I tell them that many changes would occur in their tribe and homes in their absence. They would miss the births, deaths, ceremonies, and their own puberty rites that make the life circle complete. And when the time comes to leave school, not only would home have changed, but they also would have changed. As I look at the faces I picture someone back home with the same eyes, nose, and lips. I reassure them that those kinds of schools with their harsh treatment and attitudes of "kill the Indian and save the man" have all but vanished now.

I concentrate on a photograph of a couple of Northeast Natives who are probably Mi'kmaq (fig. 181). I recognize the woman's headpiece. Both are smiling happily, a rare sight in old photographs, it seems. I ask them how the "fiddleheads" are this spring. Has the man checked the ash and done any pounding yet? Does the woman have her dyes ready for the basket material? The pair seems to share their affection openly.

Next I see three men dressed in early fancy dance regalia (fig. 182). I remember going with my parents to such dances (I like the word "dances" better than the word "powwows"), and I recall seeing the old timers dressed much like the fellows in this photo. Those gentlemen had a certain grace as they seemed to glide over the circle, bouncing just softly enough to make their bells jingle in time to the drumbeat. As the years went by, the steps changed, new songs were created, and pieces were added to the regalia. The beat went faster and faster, and "the contest was on."

182. Absaroke (Crow) Lodge Grass war dancers, from left: Edward Wolf Lays Down, Leo Bad Horse, and Bird Far Away. Crow Agency, Montana. Charles Rau Collection. N31485 (P9331)

183. The daughter and granddaughters of Bird All Over the Ground (Absaroke [Crow]). Entitled *The Story Hour*, 1917–28. Montana. Photo by Willem Wildschut. N31102

Over the years my knowledge of and respect for the songs and their meanings have remained. I still hear the elders' angry voices when a song or dance was done out of context. As the Indian world of song and dance moves into a new century, it will be interesting to see how much of this important knowledge is remembered.

In another photograph two small girls listen to a woman from a Plains tribe (fig. 183). The woman, I imagine, is an elder whose role is to teach the younger ones and to pass her wisdom to another generation. Someday these children will repeat this cycle.

My paternal grandmother was the daughter of Mexican captives, and she could speak only Kiowa. This left my brothers and me at a disadvantage in learning valuable knowledge from her. Our Kiowa graces were sadly lacking, as we must have proved to our Kiowa relations over the years. What was missing from the paternal side of our family was magnified through our maternal side. Our mother was born and raised a Delaware, and she knew very little of her father's people, who were Seminole and Creek. Her early years were hard, which was not uncommon on the southern Plains. She and her six siblings were raised in dugouts and tents until she was forced into a government boarding school at six years of age. Suddenly she was whisked off, never to return home until after her mother had died. When we children came into her life, my mother hung onto us tenaciously.

On cold winter nights she would let us all pile into bed with her, and she would tell us stories of the Delaware people that her grandmother had told to her. She told us about her life at the boarding school. I will always remember one story about her early days at the school. Since she was a "little girl" and could speak only Delaware, her dormitory duties were light. One Saturday morning the matron told my mother in English to fetch a mop, and she motioned for her to go to the basement. Mother spent the whole morning going up and down the basement stairs, bringing up everything but the mop. Each time she brought up something, the matron slapped her. When I grew older I asked my mom if she ever brought up the mop. Laughing, she said she did, and she never forgot what a mop was. Once an interviewer asked her how her people survived the Depression. Her answer was, "What Depression?" Now on winter nights I miss her warm bed and wonderful stories.

Another photograph reminds me of a similar scene (fig. 184). The Kiowa and Comanches were a nomadic people who followed the buffalo and roamed the Plains in search of food and shelter. Their raids on other tribes and non-Indian settlements were mostly to get food and horses and occasionally to take captives. Women were usually captured for procreation and to add children to the tribe. My great-grandmother was one of those children.

All this was explained to me by my father's two oldest sisters, who received all the family's respect. Both were grand women with enormous abilities to intimidate the smallest of nieces. Yet they had giant hugs that felt good and made me feel special. One of the sisters was the first Kiowa girl not only to graduate from high school but also to attend business school. Only three women could tell my dad what to do, and those aunts were two of them. When I was older I had the opportunity to share a summer with one of them. We worked hard, but at every chance she told me stories of the family.

My paternal grandfather married sisters, the only children of the original captive. He had been born in the 1860s on the southern Plains near the Wichita Mountains. He hunted, participated in war parties, and celebrated Sun Dances. He was also a scout for the army at Fort Sill. In his later life he became a sweathouse doctor and a skilled maker of bows and arrows. While he was a scout he was taught to draw on paper, and this led to his keeping a Kiowa calendar. He raised nine children with the two sisters.

My aunt told me that she would travel with her dad on horseback to visit friends and relatives and to attend celebrations. She also told me that she danced the last Ghost Dance in 1923 in her grandmother's dress. She was the last to wear the dress in the religious rite. The dress was given to me in 1969. On occasion I take it out and hold it and feel the soft skin. I think of the two

184. White Arms, (left), and Pretty
Beads (Absaroke [Crow]), ca. 1920
(?). Charles Rau Collection. N41420
(P9356)

bodies it covered in the last of the Kiowa religious practices that eventually gave way to Christianity. I remember my aunt saying how the whole family joined the Rainy Mountain Baptist Church and that the old ways were history. I liked her story, and I will always remember her as a Christian.

My first memory of buffalo involves my dad taking the family to the Wichita Mountain Wildlife Refuge near Lawton, Oklahoma (fig. 185). I know we had to go there often so my father could take pictures of them, but he also needed to sit and be near them. I think back on those times when my brothers and I were there with him. Not until later did we realize that his was the first generation who was not fully dependent on the buffalo.

An elder once told me how the buffalo came back to the southern Plains Indians. He said a

185. Albumen print of buffalo feeding on the plains, ca. 1888–93. Gelatin silver print. Photo by William R. Cross. Gen. Nelson A. Miles Collection. Presented by Maj. Sherman Miles and Mrs. Samuel Reber. P6960

186. Mary Histia (Acoma Pueblo), a potter, ca. 1900. New Mexico. N37980 (P18233)

gentleman who worked with the livestock at Fort Sill became great friends with the local Indians. He knew that the bison had been gone for more than fifty years, and the Comanches, Kiowas, and Apaches missed them terribly. He located a few American Bison in New York State and arranged to ship the animals to the Wichita Mountain Range. Great pens were erected for the buffalo. Word got out, and Indians soon camped near the pens, awaiting the arrival of the buffalo. When the buffalo did arrive, all the people wanted to do was look, and they did for days and days. As we sat with our dad gazing upon the herds, who knows what he was thinking.

This same gentleman, Mr. Frank Rush, was also responsible for bringing back what was left of the Indian celebrations. By the early 1920s the Indians had discontinued many of their traditional celebrations due to pressure from outside religions and boarding schools. The last Kiowa Sun Dance was held in 1890, and the government outlawed several other celebrations. Mr. Rush talked his Indian friends into coming to an "Indian fair." They had foot races and horse races,

187. Northern Shoshone woman winnowing grain, 1904. Lemhi reservation, Idaho. Photo by DeCost Smith. N22367

and the Indians brought their regalia out of storage. The women offered for judging the garden produce that the missionaries had taught them to grow and preserve. At last the Indian people could camp and dance together. Although this lasted only a few days each year, this was fine with them. Tourists encouraged the event. They had become familiar with Indians by watching Hollywood movies and Wild West shows. Many of the Indians chose not to participate, however, and the "Indian fair" lasted about seven years.

One photograph shows a Pueblo woman balancing a pot on her head (fig. 186). I am always fascinated by their creative use of color, especially when they paint their pottery. When I was in high school in the late 1960s, Maria Martinez came to Anadarko to visit. I had a summer job at Indian City, USA, a local tourist attraction, and she displayed a few pieces of her pottery. My dad was summoned to photograph her. As I stood in the back, she motioned for me to come to her. I had the wonderful pleasure of posing with this great woman. Not long after that visit she went with the Spirit People. Years later I visited the Research Branch of the National Museum of the American Indian in the Bronx, where I was shown a full setting of dinnerware that Mrs. Martinez had created. I could feel her presence as I did standing next to her more than three decades earlier.

For me, the photo of a woman sifting corn in the wind symbolizes tribes everywhere because corn is important to so many (fig. 187). I tell the child in the photo that I prepared corn with

188. Gallup Ceremonial, ca. 1940. Gallup, New Mexico. Photo by Rolf Tietgens. Lot 179

my mother and her sisters all my young life. I cannot imagine life without corn. I recall that necessity took my mother's older sister to the city. This left her other sister, who lived just down the road from us, to process the "squaw corn" that they had planted. During World War II when my dad and other Indian men went off to war, the women worked miracles feeding their families on their meager allotments of food. We always had gardens, and we grated, dried, pounded, and roasted corn for days. It was the children's job to keep the birds away while the corn dried on the roofs of sheds. We got to eat as much as we wanted, and we never seemed to tire of all the ways corn was prepared. The one job that my brothers and cousins all dreaded was using the old corn pounder. We all had to take a turn at this hard work, but eating the corn on cold winter days made it worth the bother. I think the best corn that I have ever eaten was with the Lenape people on the reserve at Moraviantown and Munseetown in Ontario.

The Kiowas have been invited to the Gallup Ceremonial for years (fig. 188). In 1949 my dad loaded all of us and our dog into the old sedan, and we headed west to New Mexico. On the way Dad told us stories of the Kiowa and their battle at Palo Duro Canyon near Amarillo. He told us how his father told stories of the Kiowa and Navajo fighting each other. At Gallup my dad took pictures, and I was in the parade wearing my new buckskin dress. I was pretty young then, but I remember camping south of Gallup and sleeping on the ground with my brothers between our parents. Early the next morning my mother was cooking over a fire, which was her favorite thing to do, and a Navajo couple who were herding sheep stopped by for coffee. I don't know where they came from; they just appeared. I remember eating bread that was blue and cooked on a rock at the ceremonial grounds. Before we left, my dad took pictures of my brothers and me on stuffed longhorn cows, and he bought me a little silver concho that I still have.

Searching through these photographs, I have attempted to share my life and to give some idea of the passing of time. My dad would caution that we are living too fast and that we don't know where it all will end. That statement becomes more clear to me each day. As I have passed the half-century mark now, I hear myself speaking of things in the past more than in the future. I sound like my parents. Both of them were born to Native-speaking parents, and they had the advantage of knowing their tribe's mores, humor, and simple but meaningful explanations of life. Both moved from traditional homes to modern houses, and both became Christians. An interviewer once asked me how my father knew to take photographs of his people in transition. I responded that I am sure there were times when they were painfully aware of change, especially when they looked through the fence at the buffalo. My dad just took photographs to record life, much like his father made a Kiowa calendar. My dad once said that he didn't want to be remembered for his pictures—he wanted his people to be remembered through his photographs.

As we approach the year 2000, we as Indian people can look back and learn. Through photographs we can, as never before, retrace some of our steps. I know a Kiowa gentleman named Parker McKenzie who will soon be 100. His desire is to live in three centuries, 1800, 1900, and 2000. I believe he will. He has seen his people move from tipis to houses, he has witnessed two world wars, and on television he has watched a man land on the moon. He knew people who fought against the white man in the last century and then saw their sons fight with him for this country. We have come a long way in a hundred years, and I am glad to have seen half of it. I, like Mr. McKenzie, look forward to the year 2000.

Aho, Wanishee, and mahdoe!

Photographs by
Horace Poolaw

189. From left: Elmer Buddy Saunkeah, Kaw-Au-In-Oin-Tay (Goose That Honks), and Jerry Poolaw, ca. 1928. Mount View, Oklahoma. Photo by Horace Poolaw. P2650

190. From left: Edwin "Ace" Ware, Leo "Kyco" Ware, Wanda Poolaw, Thelma Poolaw, Roloh Momaday, Vivian Saunkeah, Newton Poolaw, Eualuh Ware, Billy Tychwy, Jerry Poolaw, Cletus Poolaw, Rowena Poolaw, unidentified, Elmer "Buddy" Saunkeah, Jack Poolaw, Donald Poolaw, unidentified, Betty Poolaw, Justin Ware, ca. 1928. Outside of Pohd-Lohk's (Old Wolf, or Kiowa George) house, Mountain View, Oklahoma. Photo by Horace Poolaw. P26501

191. *From left*: Jeanette and Vanette Mopope, ca. 1928. Medicine Lodge Treaty Reinactment, Medicine Lodge, Kansas. Photo by Horace Poolaw. P26502

192. Pohd-Lohk (Old Wolf, or
Kiowa George), ca. 1928. Mountain
View, Oklahoma. Photo by Horace
Poolaw. P26503

193. From left: unidentified, Frank
Rush (organizer of the Craterville
Park Indian Fair), Pohd-Lohk (Old
Wolf, or Kiowa George), Jasper
Saunkeah, and Bruce Poolaw, ca.
1928. Craterville Park Indian Fair,
Cache, Oklahoma. Photo by Horace
Poolaw. P26504

194. Group on horseback, ca. 1928.
Pawnee Bill's Wild West Show,
Pawnee, Oklahoma. Photo by
Horace Poolaw. P26505

195. From left: Two show performers
in Pawnee Bill's Wild West Show,
Lucy "Princess Watawaso" Nicola,
and Bruce Poolaw, ca. 1928. Pawnee,
Oklahoma. Photo by Horace
Poolaw. P26506

196. Group of dancers, ca. 1928. Craterville Park Indian Fair, Cache, Oklahoma. Photo by Horace Poolaw. P26507

197. Bruce Poolaw (left, in feather headdress), and Jasper Saunkeah (right, in feather headdress), ca. 1928. Medicine Lodge Treaty Re-enactment, Medicine Lodge, Kansas. Photo by Horace Poolaw. P26508

198. From left: Lela Ware, Paul

Zumwalt, and Trecil Poolaw, ca.

1928. Mountain View, Oklahoma.

Photo by Horace Poolaw. P26509

Mrs. Lay (Seneca), 1900. Photo by

Joseph Keppler. N21273

Notes

INTRODUCTION

1. Lawrence M. Hauptman, *The Iroquois Struggle for Survival: World War II to Red Power* (Syracuse: Syracuse University Press, 1986), 243.

2. *Toronto Globe and Mail*, 3 July 1970.

3. Natasha Bonilla Martinez, "Native America in Image and Imagination: The Photography Collection," *Museum of the American Indian Newsletter* 12, no. 1 (September 1987), 2.

4. Ibid.

5. Council on Interracial Books for Children, *Chronicles of American Indian Protest* (New York: Council on Interracial Books for Children, 1979), 234.

6. Ibid. The publication of this narrative by Chief Joseph was introduced by William H. Hare, missionary bishop of Niobrara, in "An Indian's Views of Indian Affairs," *North American Review* 128 (April 1879).

7. Frederick E. Hoxie, ed., *Encyclopedia of North American Indians* (New York: Houghton Mifflin Company, 1996), 222.

8. Virginia Irving Armstrong, comp., *I Have Spoken: American History Through the Voices of the Indians* (Athens, Oh.: Swallow Press, Ohio University Press, 1971), 45; Tecumseh was speaking in July 1811.

9. Hulleah J. Tsinhnahjinnie, "Compensating Imbalances," *Exposure* 29, no. 1 (Fall 1993), 29–30.

10. Peter E. Palmquist, "Be Sure to Get a Closeup!," unpublished manuscript, 7.

11. Ibid., 10.

12. Willow Roberts Powers and Richard Hill, "Images Across Boundaries: History, Use and Ethics of Photographs of American Indians," *American Indian Cultural and Research Journal* 20, no. 3 (1996), vii.

13. Council on Interracial Books for Children, *Chronicles of American Indian Protest* (New York: Council on Interracial Books for Children, 1979), 91. This quote from Black Hawk is from his autobiography, *Life of ka-tai-me-she-kia-kiak or Black Hawk* (1834), dictated by Black Hawk in Boston.

14. Ibid, p. 201. This quote by Cochise, made during a speech in 1871 at the time of his pledge to remain at peace, appears in the *Kansas State Historical Society Collections* 13 (1915).

1. AN INDIAN AMERICAS

1. The first known photograph of a Native American, a portrait of the Reverend Peter Jones (the son of a Welshman and a Mississauga woman), was made between October 1844 and April 1845 in Great Britain by David Octavius Hill and Robert Adamson.

2. Curtis M. Hinsley and Melissa Banta, *From Site to Sight: Anthropology, Photography and the Power of Imagery* (Cambridge, Mass.: Peabody Museum of Archaeology and Ethnology, 1986), 101.

3. Clara Sue Kidwell, "Every Last Dishcloth: The Prodigious Collecting of George Gustav Heye," paper presented at the American Anthropological Association annual meeting, Washington, D.C., November 1995.

4. Ibid., 4–5.

5. James Clifford, *The Predicament of Culture: Twentieth-Century Ethnography, Literature, and Art* (Cambridge, Mass.: Harvard University Press, 1988), 213.

6. J. Alden Mason, "George G. Heye 1874–1957," *Leaflets of the Museum of the American Indian, Heye Foundation*, no. 6 (1958), 11.

7. Duane H. King, "Treasures of the Museum of the American Indian," unpublished manuscript, 11. Courtesy of Duane H. King.

8. Letters from George H. Pepper to Frederick W. Hodge, 30 June 1904 and 2 July 1904, MS.7.AAA.1.1167. Courtesy Braun Library, Southwest Museum, Los Angeles.

9. Kevin Wallace, "Slim-Shin's Monument," *New Yorker* (19 November 1960), 122.

10. Mason, "Heye," 12.

11. Hinsley and Banta, *From Site to Sight*, 108.

12. John Collier, Jr., "Photography and Visual Anthropology," in Paul Hockings, ed., *Principles of Visual Anthropology* (The Hague and Paris: Mouton Publishers, 1975), 212–13.

13. Mason, "Heye," 13.

14. Kidwell, "Every Last Dishcloth," 8, and Jorge Busadre, "Latin American Courses in the United States," in Howard F. Cline, ed., *Latin American History: Essays on its Study and Teaching, 1898–1965* (Austin: University of Texas Press, 1967), 414–18.

15. Kidwell, "Every Last Dishcloth," 9.

16. Mark R. Harrington, "Memories of My Life With George G. Heye," unpublished manuscript, NMAI Archive, OCO88/2, 1.

17. Mason, "Heye," 20.

18. Kidwell, "Every Last Dishcloth," 14.

19. Ibid., 20.

20. Wallace, "Slim-Shin's Monument," 110.

21. Annual report of the Board of Trustees of the Museum of the American Indian, Heye Foundation, to George G. Heye, curator, 1932, 8. Courtesy of the Huntington Free Library and Reading Room, Bronx, New York.

22. Letter from Jesse Nusbaum to Frederick W. Hodge, 17 October 1919, MS.7.MAI.1523. Courtesy Braun Library, Southwest Museum, Los Angeles.

23. Personal communication with Dr. Frederick J. Dockstader, MAI Director Emeritus, 19 August 1996.

24. Letter from George H. Pepper to Frederick W. Hodge, 8 October 1917, MS.7.EIC.I.145. Courtesy Braun Library, Southwest Museum, Los Angeles.

25. Alfred L. Bush and Lee Clark Mitchell, *The Photograph and the American Indian* (Princeton, N.J.: Princeton University Press, 1994), 297.

26. A. Hyatt Verrill, as told to Ruth Verrill, unpublished manuscript, NMAI Archive, OCO/32, 411.

27. Biographical information on Willem Wildschut courtesy of Stuart Conner, Billings, Montana. Anthropologist Peter Nabokov edited and published Wildschut's manuscript on noted Crow warrior Two Leggings in the 1970s.

28. Letter from Ellen Wildschut to Stuart Conner, 14 July 1972. Courtesy of Stuart Conner, Billings, Montana.

29. Wallace, "Slim-Shin's Monument," 108.

30. Annual report of the Board of Trustees of the Museum of the American Indian, Heye Foundation, to George G. Heye, curator, 1924, 11. Courtesy of the Huntington Free Library and Reading Room, Bronx, New York.

31. From George Bird Grinnell's diary for 1904–1905, entry dated 11 September 1905. Courtesy Braun Library, Southwest Museum, Los Angeles.

32. George Bird Grinnell, *The Cheyenne Indians, their history and ways of life* (Lincoln: University of Nebraska Press, 1972), 128–29.

33. From George Bird Grinnell's diary for 1904–1905, entry dated 22 October 1904. Courtesy Braun Library, Southwest Museum, Los Angeles.

34. Bush and Mitchell, *Photograph and American Indian*, 312.

35. Frederick Starr, *In Indian Mexico: A Narrative of Travel and Labor* (Chicago: Forbes and Company, 1908), 369.

36. Ibid., 398.

37. Mason, "Heye," 18.

38. Victor Wolfgang von Hagen, "The Tsátchela Indians of Western Ecuador," *Indian Notes and Monographs*, vol. 51 (New York: Museum of the American Indian, 1939), 42.

39. William H. Goetzmann and Kay Sloan, *Looking Far North: The Harriman Expedition to Alaska 1899* (New York: Viking Press, 1982), xiii, 182–83.

40. Paul Fejos, *Ethnography of the Yagua* (New York: Viking Fund, 1943), 29.

41. Personal communication with Dr. Frederick J. Dockstader, MAI Director Emeritus, 19 August 1996.

42. Ibid.

43. Ibid.

44. Tricia Hurst, "Emry Kopta (1884–1953): Each Respected the Other," *Southwest Art* 2, no. 11 (April 1982). Also see the pamphlet "Emry Kopta: The Sculptor—The Man, 1884–1953" (Taos, N.M.: Emry and Anna Kopta Foundation, 1982).

45. Marta Weigle and Barbara A. Babcock, eds. *The Great Southwest of the Fred Harvey Company and the Santa Fe Railway* (Phoenix: The Heard Museum, 1966).

46. Wallace, "Slim-Shin's Monument," 144–45.

47. Annual report of the Museum of the American Indian, Heye Foundation, 1973, 25. Courtesy of the Huntington Free Library and Reading Room, Bronx, New York,

48. Wallace, "Slim-Shin's Monument," 118.

49. George P. Horse Capture, foreword in Christopher Cardozo, ed., *Native Nations: First Americans as Seen by Edward S. Curtis* (Boston: Little, Brown and Company, Bullfinch Press, 1993), 17.

TRANSITIONS AND TRIBULATIONS

1. David M. Blackard, *Patchwork and Palmettos: Seminole-Miccosukee Folk Art Since 1820* (Fort Lauderdale, Fla.: Fort Lauderdale Historical Society, 1990), 17.

2. Betty Meggers, *Amazonia* (Washington, D.C.: Smithsonian Institution Press, 1996), 180–83.

3. Estelle Fuchs and Robert J. Havinghurst, *To Live on This Earth* (New York: Doubleday, 1972), 4, 224.

4. Sheldon Annis, *God and Production in a Guatemalan Town* (Austin: University of Texas Press, 1987), 109, 118.

5. Manning Nash, "The Social Context of Economic Choice," *Journal of the Royal Anthropological Institute* [Great Britain], (1962).

6. Barbara Tedlock and Dennis Tedlock, "Text and Textile: Language and Technology in the Arts of the Quiche Maya," *Journal of Anthropological Research* 41 (1985), 121–46.

7. Robert S. Carlson, "Discontinuous Warps: Textile Production and Ethnicity in Contemporary Highland Guatemala," in *Crafts in the World Market*, edited by June Nash (New York: State University of New York, 1993), 203.

2. CAMERA SHOTS

1. Nelson A. Miles, *Serving the Republic* (New York: Harper and Brothers Publishers, 1911), 115.

2. Jerome A. Greene, *Yellowstone Command: Colonel Nelson A. Miles and the Great Sioux War 1876–1877* (Lincoln and London: University of Nebraska Press, 1991), 18.

3. Miles, *Serving the Republic*, 139–40.

4. Ibid., 181.

5. Ibid., 228.

6. Ibid., 243.

7. Ibid., 134–35.

8. Copy of letter from President Theodore Roosevelt to Secretary of the Interior E. A. Hitchcock, 11 June 1906, NMAI Archives, OCO36/3.

9. *Granite State Free Press*, 15 November 1912.

10. Fragment of undated correspondence from Colonel Frank C. Churchill, NMAI Archives, OCO/37.1.B.

11. Personal communication with Robert Leavitt, Lebanon City Historian, Lebanon, New Hampshire, 27 September 1996.

12. Fragment of undated correspondence from Colonel Frank C. Churchill, NMAI Archives, OCO/37.1.B.

13. Manuscripts for lectures by Clara C. Churchill, NMAI Archives, OCO/38.1.B and OCO/38.2.

14. Fragment of undated correspondence from Colonel Frank C. Churchill, NMAI Archives, OCO/37.1.B.

15. Ibid.

16. Report from Colonel Frank C. Churchill to the Department of the Interior, January 1904, Moqui Training School, Keams Canon, Arizona, NMAI Archives, OC/35.3.

17. Fragment of undated correspondence from Colonel Frank C. Churchill, NMAI Archives, OCO/37.1.B.

18. Report from Colonel Frank C. Churchill on the Osage agency to the secretary of the interior, 18 April 1903, NMAI Archives, OC35, no. 3, p. 20.

19. See Kenneth W. McIntosh, *Chitto Harjo, the Crazy Snakes and the Birth of Indian Political Activism in the Twentieth Century* (Ann Arbor, Mich.: UMI, 1995) for a comprehensive history of Harjo and the Snake movement.

20. Charles Russell and Elena Quinn, eds., *Edward H. Davis and the Indians of the Southwest United States and Northwest Mexico* (Downey, Calif.: privately published by Elena Quinn), 21–30.

21. Ibid., 27.

22. Ibid., 30.

23. Ibid., 27.

24. Ibid., 103, 62.

25. Ibid., 19.

26. Letter from Edward H. Davis to George G. Heye, 16 April 1948, NMAI Archives, OC125/13.

27. Letter from Edward H. Davis to George G. Heye, 15 January 1948, NMAI Archives, OC125/13.

28. Quinn, *Edward H. Davis*, 200.

29. Edward H. Davis, "The Pursuits of a Museum Collector," *Touring Topics* (23 October 1931), 18.

30. Letter from George G. Heye to Joseph Keppler, 14 October 1946, NMAI Archives, VK-4.

31. Letter from Edward H. Davis to George G. Heye, 16 April 1948, NMAI Archives, OC125/13.

32. Diary entry describing events at Matwhy site, 28 February 1912. Edward H. Davis papers, envelope 13. Courtesy of the San Diego Historical Society, San Diego, California.

33. Curtis M. Hinsley and Melissa Banta, *From Site to Sight: Anthropology, Photography and the Power of Imagery* (Cambridge, Mass.: Peabody Museum Press, 1986), 101.

34. Judith Luskey, "Early American Anthropologists as Photographers of North American Indians," *Visual Resources* 4 (1988), 359.

35. John Witthoft, "Frank Speck: The Formative Years," *The Life and Times of Frank G. Speck 1881–1950* (Philadelphia: University of Pennsylvania, Department of Anthropology Publications in Anthropology, 1991), 2.

36. Ibid., 5.

37. Edmund S. Carpenter, "Frank Speck: Quiet Listener," *The Life and Times of Frank G. Speck 1881–1950* (Philadelphia: University of Pennsylvania, Department of Anthropology Publications in Anthropology, 1991), 83.

38. C. A. Weslager, "The Unforgettable Frank G. Speck," *The Life and Times of Frank G. Speck 1881–1950* (Philadelphia: University of Pennsylvania, Department of Anthropology Publications in Anthropology, 1991), 55.

39. William N. Fenton, "Frank G. Speck's Anthropology (1881–1950)," *The Life and Times of Frank G. Speck 1881–1950* (Philadelphia: University of Pennsylvania, Department of Anthropology Publications in Anthropology, 1991), 23–24.

40. Ibid., 25.

41. Frank Speck, "The Rappahanock Indians of Virginia," *Indian Notes and Monographs*, vol. 5, no. 3 (New York: Museum of the American Indian, 1925), viii.

42. Letter from W. A. Plecker to George L. Nelson, 8 April 1925, NMAI Archives, OC236/12.

43. Letter from Frank G. Speck to Frederick W. Hodge, 4 April 1925, NMAI Archives, OC236/12.

44. John Witthoft, "Frank Gouldsmith Speck," in John A. Garraty and Edward T. James, eds., *Dictionary of American Biography*, Supplement Four 1946–52 (New York: Charles Scribner's Sons, 1975), 762.

45. Hinsley and Banta, *From Site to Sight*, 108.

46. George W. Stocking Jr., "The Ethnographic Sensibility of the 1920s," in George W. Stocking, Jr., ed., *Romantic Motives: Essays on Anthropological Sensibility* (Madison: University of Wisconsin Press, 1989), 224.

47. Undated 1923 letter from George G. Heye to Frederick W. Hodge, MS.7.MAI.1.297, Courtesy Braun Library, Southwest Museum, Los Angeles.

48. Letter from George G. Heye to Frederick W. Hodge, 26 August 1916, MS.7.EIC.1.91, Courtesy Braun Library, Southwest Museum, Los Angles.

49. Letter from Frederick W. Hodge to George G. Heye, 11 June 1918, Southwest Museum, MS.7.HHE.1.11.; T. N. Pandey, "Anthropologists at Zuni," *Proceedings of the American Philosophical Society* 116 [need date], 330.

50. Undated 1924 letter from Zuni Indian Agency Superintendent R. J. Bauman to the Department of the Interior. Courtesy Ashiwi:Awan Museum and Heritage Center, Pueblo of Zuni, New Mexico.

3. PROCESSES AND PICTURES

1. William Welling, *Photography in America: The Formative Years 1839–1900* (New York: Thomas Y. Crowell Company, 1978), 31.

   In the daguerreotype process, a small silver-plated sheet of copper is buffed to a high polish and then placed in a light-proof box, where it is sensitized with iodine and bromide vapors. The plate is then placed in the camera and exposed. The exposed plate is developed in another box with vapors of heated mercury and subsequently fixed. The resulting image is very delicate and was usually toned with gold and placed in a small case under glass to protect its surface.

2. F. Catherwood, *Architect-Explorer of Two Worlds*, ed. Victor Wolfgang von Hagen (Barre, Mass.: Barre Publishers, 1968), 49.

3. John L. Stephens, *Incidents of Travel in Yucatan*, vol. 1 (New York: Harper & Brothers, 1843), 100–107.

4. Ibid., 174–75.

5. Catherwood, *Architect-Explorer*, 49.

6. *History of Photography* 12, no. 4 (October–December 1988), 359–63.

7. Victor Wolfgang von Hagen, *Maya Explorer, John Lloyd Stephens and the Lost Cities of Central America and Yucatán* (San Francisco: Chronicle Books, 1990), 255.

8. Don D. Nibbelink, "The First Governmental Application of Photography," *Journal of the Franklin Institute*, no. 236 (September 1943), 265–71.

9. Gail Buckland, *First Photographs* (New York: Macmillan Publishing Co., 1980), 39.

10. Richard D. Altick, *The Shows of London* (Cambridge, Mass.: Belknap Press, Harvard University Press, 1978), 275–79.

11. Daguerreotypes of Maungwudaus (George Henry) and his fellow Ojibwe are in the Chicago Historical Society, the Public Archives of Canada, the George Eastman House, and private collections.

12. *Exploring with Fremont, Private Diaries of Charles Preuss, etc.*, trans. and ed. Edwin G. and Elizabeth K. Gudde (Norman: University of Oklahoma Press, 1958), 32.

13. Ibid., 35.

14. S. N. Carvalho, *Incidents of Travel and Adventure in the Far West; with Col. Fremont's Last Expedition* (New York: Derby & Jackson, 1857), 32–33.

15. Ibid. pp. 67–68

16. Congressional Journal, 36th Congress, 1st session, Executive Document no. 56, 1860, 103.

17. Commonwealth of Massachusetts, "Statistical Information Relating to Certain Branches of Industry in Massachusetts for the Year Ending June 1, 1855" (Boston, 1856), 591.

18. Reprint of Glover's letter of 29 July 1866 in *Philadelphia Photographer* (December 1866), 367–68.

19. Ibid., 339.

20. Need reference citation.

21. William H. Jackson and Howard R. Driggs, *The Pioneer Photographer* (Yonkers, N.Y.: World Book Company, 1929), 58–60.

22. Letter from Russell dated 3 July 1869 to the *Nunda News*; quoted in Weston J. Naef and James N. Wood, *Era of Exploration* (Boston: New York Graphic Society, 1975), 203.

23. William Culp Darrah, *Stereo Views* (Gettysburgh, Penn.: Times and News Publishing Co., 1964), 75, 85.

24. Letter of September 15, printed in *Anthony's Photographic Bulletin* 3 (November 1872), 746–47.

25. Letter from Joseph Henry to Lewis V. Bogy, Commissioner of Indian Affairs, dated 20 February 1867, now in the National Archives and quoted in Paula Richardson Fleming and Judith Luskey, *The North American Indians in Early Photographs* (New York: Barnes & Noble Books, 1986), 22–23.

26. Lee Moorhouse, "Indian Photography," *American Annual of Photography* (New York: Anthony and Scovill Company, 1904), 77–83.

27. Ibid.

28. Speech given by Curtis in 1906 reprinted in Mick Gidley, "Edward S. Curtis Speaks . . .," *History of Photography* 2, no. 4 (October 1978), 349–50.

29. Ibid., 352.

30. Ibid.

4. DEVELOPED IDENTITIES

1. O. O. Howard, *Famous Indian Chiefs I Have Known* (Lincoln: University of Nebraska Press, 1989), 302.

2. Oglala Lakota chief Long Wolf died in 1892 while on tour with Buffalo Bill's Wild West Show, and was buried in London. In 1995, Long Wolf's descendants finally located his grave when Elizabeth Knight of Bromsgrove, England, wrote to *Indian Country Today* seeking information on the chief after reading of his burial in a London cemetery in a 1920 essay by Scottish adventurer Robert C. Graham. Long Wolf's family eventually returned his remains to South Dakota in 1997.

3. Olga Kaltenborn, "Interprets Racial Types," *Brooklyn Eagle*, 2 January 1927.

4. Jeffery Stewart, *To Color America: Portraits by Winhold Reiss* Washington, D.C.: Smithsonian Institution Press, 1989), 72.

5. Alfred Crosby, "Virginia Soil Epidemics as a Factor in the Aboriginal Depopulation of America," *William and Mary Quarterly* 33, 3d ser. (1976), 299.

5. SPIRIT CAPTURE

1. Horace Monroe Poolaw (1906–1984) worked as a photographer from 1920 to 1975 and taught photography during World War II.

Selected Bibliography

Altick, Richard D. *The Shows of London.* Cambridge, Mass.: Harvard University Press, Belknap Press, 1978.

Annis, Sheldon. *God and Production in a Guatemalan Town.* Austin: University of Texas Press, 1987.

Barrett, S. M., ed. *Geronimo's Story of His Life.* New York, Duffield and Co., 1906.

Blackard, David M. *Patchwork and Palmettos: Seminole-Miccosukee Folk Art Since 1820.* Fort Lauderdale, Fla.: Fort Lauderdale Historical Society, 1990.

Buckland, Gail. *First Photographs: People, Places and Phenomena As Captured for the First Time by the Camera.* New York: Macmillan Publishing, 1980.

Bush, Alfred L., and Lee Clark Mitchell. *The Photograph and the American Indian.* Princeton, N.J.: Princeton University Press, 1994.

Carlson, Robert S. "Discontinuous Warps: Textile Production and Ethnicity in Contemporary Highland Guatemala." In June C. Nash, ed. *Crafts in the World Market.* Albany State University of New York Press, 1993.

Carpenter, Edmund S. "Frank Speck: Quiet Listener." In Roy Blankenship, ed. *The Life and Times of Frank G. Speck, 1881–1950.* Philadelphia: University of Pennsylvania Press, 1991.

Carvalho, S. N. *Incidents of Travel and Adventure in the Far West, with Col. Fremont's Last Expedition.* New York: Derby and Jackson, 1857.

Chronicles of American Indian Protest. New York: Council on Interracial Books for Children, 1979.

Clifford, James. *The Predicament of Culture: Twentieth-Century Ethnography, Literature and Art.* Cambridge, Mass.: Harvard University Press, 1988.

Collier, John, Jr. "Photography and Visual Anthropology." In Paul Hockings, ed. *Principles of Visual Anthropology.* The Hague and Paris: Mouton Publishers, 1975.

Collier, John, Jr., and Malcolm Collier. *Visual Anthropology: Photography as a Research Method.* Albuquerque: University of New Mexico Press, 1986.

Darrah, William Culp. *Stereo Views: A History of Stereographs in America and Their Collection.* Gettysburg, Penn.: Times and News Publishing Company, 1964.

Davis, Edward H. "The Pursuits of a Museum Collector." *Touring Topics* 23, no. 10 (October 1931), 16–21; 35–36.

Emry Kopta: The Sculptor—The Man, 1884–1953. Taos, N. Mex.: Emry and Anna Kopta Foundation, 1982.

Fejos, Paul. *Ethnography of the Yagua.* New York: The Viking Fund Inc., 1943.

Fenton, William N. "Frank G. Speck's Anthropology (1881–1950)." In Roy Blankenship, ed. *The Life and Times of Frank G. Speck, 1881–1950.* Philadelphia: University of Pennsylvania Press, 1991.

Fleming, Paula Richardson, and Judith Luskey. *The North American Indians in Early Photographs.* New York: Barnes and Noble Books, 1986.

Fuchs, Estelle, and Robert J. Havinghurst. *To Live on This Earth.* Garden City, N.Y.: Doubleday, 1972.

Gidley, Mike. "Edward S. Curtis Speaks. . . ." *History of Photography* 2, no. 4 (October 1978): 77–83.

Goetzmann, William H., and Kay Sloan. *Looking Far North: The Harriman Expedition to Alaska 1899.* New York: Viking Press, 1982.

Greene, Jerome A. *Yellowstone Command: Colonel Nelson A. Miles and the Great Sioux War, 1876–1877.* Lincoln: University of Nebraska Press, 1991.

Gudde, Edwin G., and Elizabeth K. Gudde, trans. and ed. *Exploring with Fremont: Private Diaries of Charles Preuss.* Norman: University of Oklahoma Press, 1958.

Hanson, David A. "The Beginnings of Photographic Reproduction in the USA," *History of Photography* 12, no. 4 (October–December 1988): 357–76.

Harrington, Mark R. "Memories of My Life with George G. Heye," unpublished manuscript, OCO88/2, National Museum of the American Indian Archives.

Hauptman, Lawrence M. *The Iroquois Struggle for Survival: World War II to Red Power.* Syracuse, N.Y.: Syracuse University Press, 1986.

Hinsley, Curtis M., and Melissa Banta. *From Site to Sight: Anthropology, Photography, and the Power of Imagery.* Cambridge, Mass.: Peabody Museum Press, 1986.

Horse Capture, George P. Foreword in Christopher Cardozo, ed. *Native Nations: First Americans as Seen by Edward S. Curtis.* Boston: Little, Brown and Company, Bullfinch Press, 1993.

Hoxie, Fredrick E., ed. *Encyclopedia of North American Indians.* Boston: Houghton Mifflin Company, 1996.

Hurst, Tricia. "Emry Kopta (1884–1953): Each Respected the Other." *Southwest Art* 2, no. 11 (April 1982): 84–91.

Jackson, William H., and Howard R. Driggs. *The Pioneer Photographer: Rocky Mountain Adventures with a Camera.* Yonkers, N.Y.: World Book Company, 1929.

Kidwell, Clara Sue. "Every Last Dishcloth: The Prodigious Collecting of George Gustav Heye," unpublished manuscript of paper presented at the American Anthropological Association annual meeting, Washington, D.C., November 1995.

King, Duane H. "Treasures of the Museum of the American Indian," unpublished manuscript.

Luskey, Judith. "Early American Anthropologists as Photographers of North American Indians." *Visual Resources* 4 (winter 1988): 359–72.

Mason, J. Alden. "George G. Heye, 1874–1957," *Leaflets of the Museum of the American Indian, Heye Foundation,* no. 6 (New York, 1958).

McIntosh, Kenneth W. *Chitto Harjo, the Crazy Snakes and the Birth of Indian Political Activism in the Twentieth Century.* Ann Arbor, Mich.: UMI, 1993.

Meggers, Betty. *Amazonia: Man and Culture in a Counterfeit Paradise.* Washington, D.C.: Smithsonian Institution Press, 1996.

Miles, Nelson A. *Serving the Republic.* New York: Harper and Brothers Publishers Company, 1911.

Moorhouse, Lee. "Indian Photography." In Spencer B. Hord, ed. *The American Annual of Photography and Photographic Times-Bulletin Almanac, 1904.*

(New York: Anthony and Scovill Company, 1904): 77–83.

Naef, Weston J., and James N. Wood. *Era of Exploration: The Rise of Landscape Photography in the American West.* Boston: New York Graphic Society, 1975.

Nash, Manning. "The Social Context of Economic Choice in a Small Society." *Journal of the Royal Anthropological Institute* 61 (Great Britain, 1962): 186–191.

Nibbelink, Don D. "The First Governmental Application of Photography." *Journal of the Franklin Institute,* no. 236 (September 1943): 265–71.

Palmquist, Peter E. "Be Sure to Get a Good Close-up!" unpublished manuscript.

Pandey, T. N. "Anthropologists at Zuni." *Proceedings of the American Philosophical Society* 116, no. 4 (1972): 321–37.

"Photographic Reproduction in the USA." *History of Photography* 12, no. 4 (October–December 1988): 359–63.

Powers, Willow Roberts and Richard Hill, eds. "Images Across Boundaries: History, Use and Ethics of Photographs of American Indians," *American Indian Culture and Research Journal* 20, no. 3 (1996): 129–36.

Quinn, Charles Russell, and Elena Quinn, eds. *Edward H. Davis and the Indians of the Southwest United States and Northwest Mexico.* Privately published by Elena Quinn, Downey, Calif., 1965.

Sheehan, Edward R. F. *Agony in the Garden: A Stranger in Central America.* Boston: Houghton Mifflin and Company, 1989.

Speck, Frank. "The Rappahanock Indians of Virginia." *Indian Notes and Monographs* 5, no. 3 (New York: Museum of the American Indian, 1925): 19–83.

Starr, Fredrick. *In Indian Mexico: A Narrative of Travel and Labor.* Chicago: Forbes and Company, 1908.

Stevens, John L. *Incidents of Travel in Yucatan.* Vol. 1. New York: Harper and Brothers Publishing Company, 1843.

Stocking, George W., Jr., ed. *Romantic Motives: Essays on Anthropological Sensibility.* Madison: University of Wisconsin Press, 1989.

Tedlock, Barbara, and Dennis Tedlock. "Text and Textile: Language and Technology in the Arts of Quiche Maya." *Journal of Anthropological Research* 41 (1985): 121–46.

Tsinhnahjinnie, Hulleah J. "Compensating Imbalances." *Exposure* 29, no. 1 (Fall 1993): 29–30.

von Hagen, Victor Wolfgang. *Frederick Catherwood, Architect-Explorer of Two Worlds.* Barre, Mass.: Barre Publishers, 1968.

_____. *Maya Explorer: John Lloyd Stephens and the Lost Cities of Central America and Yucatán.* San Francisco: Chronicle Books, 1990.

Wallace, Kevin. "A Reporter at Large: Slim-Shin's Monument." *New Yorker* 36 (19 November 1960): 104–146.

Welling, William. *Photography in America: The Formative Years, 1839–1900.* New York: Thomas Y. Crowell Company, 1978.

Weslager, C. A. "The Unforgettable Frank G. Speck." In Roy Blankenship, ed. *The Life and Times of Frank G. Speck, 1881–1950.* Philadelphia: University of Pennsylvania Press, 1991.

Wilson, James Grant, and John Fiske, eds. *Appleton's Cyclopaedia of American Biography.* New York: D. Appleton and Company, 1887–88.

Witthoft, John. "Frank Speck: The Formative Years." In Roy Blankenship, ed. *The Life and Times of Frank G. Speck, 1881–1950.* Philadelphia: University of Pennsylvania Press, 1991.

Montagnais men fishing, 1958.

Photo by William F. Stiles. N41174

Contributors

PAMELA DEWEY, Head of the Photo Archive at the National Museum of the American Indian, is a former adjunct instructor in video art at her alma mater, New York University. A photographer and textile artist whose works have appeared in many public shows, Ms. Dewey is also a curator of art exhibitions.

KATHERINE FOGDEN (Mohawk) is a photographer in the Photo Archive of the National Museum of the American Indian. She has previously worked as an assistant curator and gallery manager at the American Indian Community House Art Gallery, and has shown her photographic work in numerous exhibitions.

DOROTHY GRANDBOIS (Turtle Mountain Chippewa) is an award-winning photographer and alumna of the Institute of American Indian Arts. At the age of five, she was sent away from home and attended both Catholic and government boarding schools, experiences that still influence her photographic work.

LARRY GUS (Navajo) is a freelance editorial and studio photographer based in Los Angeles. His work, which is highly respected among Native editors, has appeared in numerous Native publications and also mainstream newspapers, including the *Los Angeles Times*.

RICHARD W. HILL, SR. (Tuscarora), former special assistant to the director at the National Museum of the American Indian, is a professor of American Studies at the State University of New York at Buffalo. He is a leading authority on contemporary Native American art and Indian images in artworks and on film. Mr. Hill has also worked as museum director and principal designer of the new Institute of American Indian Arts Museum in Santa Fe, New Mexico, and was museum director of the Native American Center for the Living Arts.

TIM JOHNSON (Mohawk), Deputy Assistant Director for Community Services at the National Museum of the American Indian, is a photojournalist and editor who has reported extensively on a wide range of indigenous peoples' issues, including economics, ecology, land claims, agriculture, spirituality, health, social science, sports, and medicine. Before his current posting, he was executive manager for communications and business development of Akwe:kon Press, Cornell University, and the cofounder of *Native Americas* journal. A founding board member of the Native Indian/Inuit Photographers' Association, Mr. Johnson has also worked with Plenty Canada, an indigenous international development organization, where he edited the book *Echoes of the Ancestors* (1993). He has also lectured in the department of communications at Buffalo State College, and created *Turtle Quarterly*, an award-winning museum magazine dealing with Native arts, histories, and contemporary cultures.

JANINE SARNA JONES is a photo archive specialist in the Photo Archive of the National Museum of the American Indian. She began working with images of Native people while attending Stanford University, where she participated in the Horace Poolaw Photography Project. Ms. Sarna Jones is currently assisting in the development of the Photo Archive's digital image database.

NATASHA BONILLA MARTINEZ is the foremost expert on the Photo Archive of the National Museum of the American Indian. She is largely credited with building the department through independent fundraising that supported new research, documentation, and public programming for the collections during her eight-year tenure as Assistant Curator of Photography, when the collections were housed by the Museum of the American Indian, Heye Foundation. Ms. Bonilla Martinez is the sole proprietor of ¡Cultura Works!, a museum consulting service.

LARRY McNEIL (Tlingit) is a studio and editorial photographer who has taught photography at the Institute of American Indian Arts in Santa Fe, New Mexico, and is president of the Native Indian/Inuit Photographers' Association. His photography has appeared in numerous exhibitions and publications.

LAURA NASH is a former curatorial assistant for photography in the Photo Archive of the National Museum of the American Indian, where she worked with researchers, scholars, publishers, and Native American community representatives to research and locate images from the Archive.

LINDA POOLAW (Delaware–Kiowa), a photographic researcher and former Stanford University instructor, was born in an Indian Health hospital in Oklahoma. Her father, Horace Poolaw, was a Kiowa photographer who worked as a guard in a munitions plant during WWII. Interest in her father's photographs led her to complete extensive research and study on that body of work, which documents many transitions of Indian peoples. Ms. Poolaw continues to research and study the changing Indian world, often working with Native elders through discussion and sometimes ceremony to gain important information on archival photographs.

NIGEL RUSSELL is curator of The Spira Collection, New York, where he oversees cataloguing a collection of approximately 20,000 items relating to the history of photography. He has also worked as an antiques dealer specializing in photographic memorabilia, and as a manager and cataloguer at Sotheby's in New York and London.

ROSE WYACO (Zuni) is an ethnographic researcher who has done extensive research on Zuni images in the Hendricks-Hodge photographic collection of National Museum of the American Indian Photo Archive. She has also conducted research on Zuni materials at the Smithsonian's National Museum of Natural History, and was the founding director of the A:shiwi A:wan Museum and Heritage Center in Zuni, New Mexico.

Index

Seneca boy in longhouse kitchen, 1907. Photo by Mark R. Harrington. N2635